Staying Sane

In the Veterinary Profession

by

Annette Docsway, DVM

Copyright 2019

"Survival is the ability to swim in strange waters."
- Frank Herbert

Dedicated to those we have lost
and to those who continue to survive

"Just keep swimming."
- Dory

Table of Contents

Foreword……………………………………1	Sequential Cartoons……………………183
My "Career"……………………………7	Other DVMs……………………………197
Dear Younger and Less-Grey Me…………20	The Vet With The Pet…………………201
Suicide and Mental Health………………24	Clientese………………………………209
Clients……………………………………50	Practice Tips……………………………213
Client Expectations………………………83	Veterinary Truisms……………………224
Client Loyalty…………………………100	Prescriptions……………………………227
Client Perceptions……………………102	Veterinary Bingo………………………233
Clients As Children……………………122	Reverse Clinic Survey…………………235
Money……………………………………124	Jaded Vet Quiz…………………………238
Insults……………………………………143	Computer/Scheduling Entries…………241
Reviews…………………………………146	Pet Names………………………………244
Divorce Letters…………………………149	Pet Names Part 2………………………247
Judging…………………………………151	Client Comments………………………250
Euthanasia………………………………153	Afterword………………………………261
Convenience Euthanasia………………154	
Products That Kill……………………159	
The Vet Tech That Everyone Knows……163	
Human-Animal Bond……………………164	
General…………………………………166	

Foreword

I'm probably the last person to give advice. If you're reading this book, perhaps I am your last resort. I feel, sometimes, that my advice works only for me; it makes me uncomfortable to give advice to others. Giving advice feels like the height of hubris. However, I've found when I share my thoughts, other people find value in them. Therefore, I'm going against my nature here.

I try to avoid the regular, travel-worn advice, because it can be found in so many other places. I try to avoid clichés and easy answers because I think they gloss over the difficulties, like putting a band-aid on a fracture. There is a lot in our profession that defies easy answers. Some of my advice may not be for you. That's okay. However, I feel everyone should have different examples to choose from when trying to wrestle with the myriad hardships they'll encounter in the veterinary profession. And when I look around, I see a lot of advice being given that isn't right for me. You have to find the right approach that works for you, the approach that feels most natural for your personality.

Unfortunately, this tends to mean we each have to reinvent the wheel for ourselves and our careers. That's what makes this so hard. No one can tell you the exact right way to approach this job. I'm hoping that the questionable "wisdom" you find here might be helpful to you. A lot of my advice is not necessarily in how to make things "right", but how situations impact you personally and how viewing them through a certain prism might lessen their negative power. I'm hoping this book helps the learning curve not be as steep for navigating a typical tumultuous career. I feel like I'm the person who points out the poop-piles hiding in the dark so you don't fully step in them but maybe just catch it on the edge where it's easier to scrape off. I also feel like the person who makes inappropriate analogies.

My background is small animal medicine, so please forgive my niche approach. Hopefully, some of the advice I have to offer translates into other aspects of the profession or life in general. At the time of this writing, I have put in twenty-five years since graduation, but it hardly feels like more than a hundred.

Much of this book will also be from an introvert's view. It seems there are plenty of extroverts out there who promulgate positivity, smiling more often, making gratitude journals, meditation, getting out and doing things. They're well-meaning and if those things work for you then I'm happy. I've found them to not be very helpful. For me, they feel forced. After I had shared how awkward small-talk is for me with clients, someone told me, "You just need to decide to like people." And my first thought was, "Have you met *people*?" Another instance - scheduling events to relieve stress into an already full schedule, as most of us have due to the nature of the job, seems like advice that just adds to the stress. Now you're stressed because you can't get to the things you feel you need to do to relieve stress. Again, you have to find the middle-ground that works and feels natural to you. I find it a personal success to just put one foot in front of the other each and every day.

Another caveat. When I talk about clients and owners, I'm painting with a broad brush. Not all clients are going to be difficult or unreasonable. Many, yes, but not all. It may seem I'm accusing all clients, but I'm not. You'll have amazing clients – those that listen, those that care, those that follow your advice. Treasure them. Make sure you appreciate the former, because they deserve recognition. This book is here to try to help you deal with those other clients.

One of the things I've noticed in advice about dealing with stress is we assume that a stress level of 11 is acceptable; we just need to develop an approach that allows us to deal with that. Nowhere have I seen advice where we reject that assumption. We need to have an environment, a profession where it is okay to have a lower level of stress, whether that comes from external or personal internal forces. Aiming for a life-work balance of stress between 4 or 7 may mean you aren't able to do anything and everything you want or feel you need to do in the job, but that's ok. It is acceptable and more sustainable than trying to manage a stress level of 11 down to a 9.8. And let's be honest, you can't have a life stress level of zero without being in a coma, so that's not a goal here either. You'll find some of my advice is geared not to make everything perfect, but making the argument that the imperfect will happen; it's how we learn to identify and deal with those moments that will see us through.

My spouse says I should be more positive. I'm positive the situations I discuss in this book will happen, with variation, to you. I think we ignore much of the negative at our peril. We can't slap a happy mask on and call it good. The yelling client will happen, the closely managed case will fail. I object to the false narrative that all negativity can be done away with if we just handle things exactly and properly. I think that's the advice I hear a lot that just adds to our already full cup of stressors. It puts too much pressure on us. As if we can control everything – the vagaries of disease processes, client compliance and education. For example, read any advice magazine where they have what they deem the "perfect" way to talk to an owner to obtain consent and compliance. They read so stilted and false I have to assume they're written by people who haven't done this job. They're written as if the owner you're talking to is a reasonable person motivated to helping their pet, when much of the time they aren't. The implication is, if you don't get a positive response from an owner, the fault lies with you, if only you'd tried harder. And that's simply not true. Regular advice will say you have to understand the pressures the client is under and tailor the conversation in such a way as to incorporate their fears and resistance. My viewpoint is that is way more work and effort than I am capable of; it is literally beyond my capacity to read a person that well. Our job is to convey information and give advice to the best of our ability. The client's job is to listen and hopefully respond appropriately. When they don't? It is not your fault. Whereas regular advice puts more pressure on you to do a better job, it doesn't acknowledge the intangibles that you have no control over. My advice, which some may deem negative, tries to take the pressure off of you and obtain a viewpoint that cushions you from self-recrimination; it's the Fifth Amendment of the Veterinary Code. Look it up. I acknowledge the negative side and then try to mitigate its impact. This may sound like just another way of spinning a positive, but hopefully I'll give enough examples, you'll get what I'm saying.

I will be bringing up a lot of the adverse situations that you may have to deal with in this job.

I do this not to wallow, but to inform. Forewarned is forearmed. I wish I had been. It would have saved a lot of hand-wringing and self-doubt. If you encounter a situation in practice, I hope this book will cause you to think, "Ooooohhh, so this is what they meant." and you'll be better prepared to deal with it.

On that note, I'd like to say, you will have amazing days and great clients. You will have unexpected successes and feel great joy at times. You will work with helpful colleagues and have fantastic staff. Just because I don't spend any time talking about those things, does not mean I don't acknowledge and understand their value. I simply feel those things take care of themselves. They are their own reward. The point of this book is to help with those other times. You must be made aware of what bad event(s) may happen in advance to have a proper response to when they occur. You will also be stronger for the knowledge, for you will realize it happens to everyone and is not a fault in your approach or personality. Just as this book may not be necessary to those who have it figured out, I want to help what I think is the majority of us that are trying to accrue as little damage as possible as we muddle through the day.

One final disclosure; while I would like to say I *am* a veterinarian, it is more accurate to say that being a veterinarian is what I do. I believe I do it well and I certainly try every day to do my best. However, it is a job. It is not how I define myself. I think that is another area that causes unfortunate pain for us. From pre-vet through entry into the profession, we define ourselves as becoming veterinarians. For some of us, the reality is disheartening and disillusioning. I think many of us are ill-prepared for that fracturing and we suffer unduly. I do my job well. I am not less of a veterinarian because I don't view it as a vocation or a calling; it's a job. This book is here to hopefully give you a framework that makes your life and job easier.

The Heavy Stuff

My "Career"

Another thing I hate to do is talk about myself. This is a conundrum, because I feel compelled to do so since I think my history can be illustrative of how many of us approached this profession and then what it became as we spent more time in it. I'll let you be the judge.

We all get asked, "When did you know you wanted to be a vet?" And that's a tough one for me. I remember being about three months old. Understand I was very advanced for my age; I was being read to at a six-month old level. It was a Tuesday afternoon. I'd just been fed and changed, feeling content with the universe, and I thought, "I think I'll be a veterinarian when I grow up." I'll warn you now, at three months of age your cognitive abilities are not sufficiently advanced to be making firm long-term life decisions such as this. But there I was.

I kid. Slightly. I might have been two months old. The point is the goal has always been there. It'd be like trying to answer, "When did you become right-handed?" or "When did you decide to have brown eyes?" And I think that innate feeling might be true for many of us. We were doomed young. I kid again. Slightly.

I did one of those career planning profiles in my freshman year of high school. They're designed to help guide you in determining what you are able to do, what you want to do, and what you are capable of doing. Having known I wanted to be a veterinarian since I was a blastula, I felt the whole thing was a waste of time. Did it anyway. Here was the top 10 list of occupations that my answers about interests, grades, and other minutiae generated:

1) Clergy/Religious Worker
2) Dentist
3) Physician/Doctor
4) Physical Therapist
5) Occupational Therapist
6) Speech Pathologist
7) Interpreter/Translator
8) Chiropractor
9) Optometrist
10) Teacher, Elementary or Secondary

Not one sign of veterinarian on that list. I took this to mean that the whole thing was invalid. *Now*, of course, I think it might have been trying to tell me something. Maybe like some cryptic warning. If you look at it a certain way, the vet school educational process is kind of like a horror movie: Last Vet School On the Left or Texas Vet School Massacre or Night of the Living Vet Student. Perhaps the profile was accurate, just not specific. After all, most of them are medically related; it's just as soon as you cancel out wanting to work on human beings, they all drop out. Which, I realize is ironic, considering the all-too-intimate dealings with people we have forced on us on a daily basis.

I was a typical pre-vet. I could not be dissuaded by any facts. Not that, honestly too many people tried outside of a tepid, "Are you sure?" Everything I did was geared toward getting into vet school. And what I had to go through seems to pale in comparison with what I see pre-vets putting themselves through now. I think the obstacles to vet school inadvertently select for a certain personality type – driven, focused, insane work ethic, intelligent, perfectionist. Binding these traits is a through-line of empathy that serves as the engine of motivation. How many of us castigated ourselves for "B"s? Seems ridiculous to me now, but the system is set up to make us think that unless we have a 6.2 GPA, a 1900 SAT score, and a 600 cumulative GRE, we might not get into vet school. And getting into vet school was our single most important goal in life, right? It's how we defined ourselves. You know I'm exaggerating those scores above, but it felt that way didn't it? The level of competition to get into vet school has only gotten worse since my day.

An aside about the bane that inorganic chemistry played on my pre-vet brain. Took an advanced college-level course in senior year of high school and received a "C". This is terrible for any pre-vet. It made me want to have a flare-gun in my locker (please feel free to look up this reference). Before attending Arizona State, I figured I'd take the same course at a community college. Received a "C". Ok, then. Took it at ASU. Received a "C". Not happy about this, but it finally got through my stubborn pre-vet mind that further pushing would not make the result change. I fretted how much that might affect my chances to get into vet school. Which, yes, now over thirty-five years later is laughable, but at the time seemed life or death. This was one of my first lessons in appreciating that, to be a vet does not infer that we have to be great at everything. Neither should we believe so.

Do you know how many volunteer or medical experience hours someone applying to medical school needs? Zero. Think about that for a moment and wonder why vet school is so different. Why is this requirement so emphasized? After all, if you're inclined to go to vet school, you're going to be surrounding yourself with animals anyway. It seems unnecessary. It reinforces the belief later in life that you need to volunteer your time and do things for free. It conveys that your time is not worth anything except as an admittance ticket.

And vet school requirements only make it worse. On one school's site they list required volunteer or animal experience of 500 hours, but then go on to say that most applicants have over 2,000 hours. Well, which is it? This sends pre-vets into a frenzy that just feeds on itself because they're out there thinking, "I'll get 3,000 hours then!" It also doesn't help that the population chosen for admission seems to be pretty arbitrary. That's because they're also based on intangibles such as letters of recommendation and interviews and what qualities the particular school wants in an incoming class; things an applicant has little control over.

There's a "spur or deter" debate in the profession. Do we help spur pre-vets in their endeavors or do we try to deter? I take a middle approach. I try to educate them as to what they will face. That might seem like "deter", but I think one of the things we don't do well for pre-vets and veterinary students is prepare them adequately to enter the profession. Yes, we do an amazing job of educating, of emphasizing the minutiae, of academically flogging them through the hoops. But personal, mental, financial, emotional, spiritual growth and fortitude?

You know, the things that make us a whole person, not just a veterinarian? Nope. Nowhere to be seen or discussed. When they get into the profession they are ill-prepared for the interpersonal drama of clinic practice, of dealing with the beast known as "the public", the hours, the doubt, the general lack of support in the community.

It took me two attempts to get into vet school. I went to the school and asked what I could do to improve my chances for the second attempt. I was told my GRE scores weren't the best (if I remember correctly, they were mid 70% for each of the categories). I called the GRE people and asked what I could do to improve my score and was told that the test is geared toward your I.Q., therefore there isn't much that can be done to substantially alter your score. I was a pre-vet. I wasn't going to let anything like logic stand in my way, having completely forgotten the inorganic chemistry lesson. I studied more. Ended up getting mid-90% in all categories. That and the fact that I was employed as a glorified janitor (my official title was Wiper of Animals' Bottoms) at the school's research facility is what I'm sure got me an interview. In the interview, the only substantial question they asked was, "How do you explain the increase in your score between the first and second GRE?" Thinking back to what I'd been told, I answered, "I got smarter." I guess you could say I got accepted, in part, by being a smartass. Little did they know they were only rewarding my behavior.

There needs to be a more considered approach to what we ask of pre-vets. When the system tells you to check off all of these distinct academic boxes, and then relies on intangibles, expecting people to be this vague definition called "well-rounded", we're setting many people up to put in a great deal of time and effort to fail and have disappointment through no fault of their own. The definition of people who do get in is mostly going to be people who aren't "well-rounded"; after all, everything they've done has been at the behest of the requirements put before them and the pressures they've put on themselves to please some ill-defined veterinary silhouette. The selection of the empathetic-perfectionist behavior, which served us so well upon getting in to vet school, is the same behavior that ends up working against us once we're in practice.

Vet school does nothing to alleviate this. In fact, they tend to double-down on expectations. I know things are changing and there is more awareness of the stressors students suffer under, but I think more needs to be done. I knew vet school would be difficult. I'm sure we all did. However, what I didn't expect was that the staff, administration, and faculty would make things more arduous. I joked that they only had a parasympathetic nervous system. And that "student support" was an oxymoron. I found the school as a whole to be uncaring whether you learned or not, unsupportive, and sometimes downright antagonistic. If you couldn't do it on your own, well, that wasn't their problem. As one professor told me, "You need to try harder." Oh, so helpful. Want to know where imposter syndrome comes from? Look no further than vet school. Condescension by professors, residents, and clinicians reinforces insecurity in your abilities. Do your absolute best, even come through positively with a case or answer, and they will still find something to nitpick or deride. And they expect you to go out into the world and perform after contributing nothing to your confidence or morale. Come on! We're really bright, hard-working people that the school chose! And then we're treated as if nothing we do is correct, where the slightest misstep or misunderstanding is treated as an egregious sin. At a minimum I never heard encouragement or guidance from anyone at the school.

My father passed away from a lethal combination of COPD and Legionella infection near the end of my third year. It happened to fall during the week of spring break, so I had no interruption in my school schedule, but it also left no time for grieving in any proper manner. By this time the administration vacillated between uncaring to hostile in their attitude and I felt I couldn't show any weakness or lessened effort without consequences. The main thing I wanted to share here, however, is what my father said to me on the phone, at a time I didn't realize they'd be the last words I heard from him. He knew I was having a tough time in school and life and he said, "You can only do your best." I have taken that to heart in the rest of my life because as simple as it is, it's true. So often we cause ourselves angst by trying to be someone else's best. We compare ourselves to others and feel compelled to compete at their level or feel we are somehow less because we can't operate at their level. Our pre-vet and vet school experiences compound this attitude. Vet school is very narrow-minded in its academic definition of what being a good veterinarian is.

I'm going to tell you right now, those people you're comparing yourself too can't operate at your level. Everyone has strengths and weaknesses. Everyone. We have to admit to ourselves that it is ok to not be amazing at everything. Those you admire? They're not amazing at everything, no matter what you may think. I guarantee you that there are others that look enviably upon you and what you can do. We don't give ourselves enough credit. We can only be ourselves. We can only do our best. You can't do someone else's best; it's enough to do yours.

I did four years of undergraduate school, culminating in a BS in Zoology and a laudable GPA of 3.65. Feeling pretty good about myself. Feeling like the big brains! I graduated vet school with a GPA of 2.65. By the way, this makes me a BS DVM; it's on all my business cards. So it's ok to be skeptical with what I have to say. You know that joke, "What do they call the person who graduates last in their vet school class?" For my school, the punchline wasn't "doctor", it was my name. I can admit this now because it's so far in my past. But I'll admit to being ashamed and embarrassed at what seemed a failing. They switch up the rules from being a well-rounded individual then hinge everything on your grades and test-taking abilities. Understand, no one cares about your grades once you graduate vet school. Not one client has inquired, as I dispense ocular medication, what my grade was in Ophthalmology. Your GPA is not reflective of who you are. I would even posit that it is a poor reflection of your intelligence and abilities. There's so much sheer unnecessary antiquated crap thrown at you in vet school that is completely useless in a practice setting, yet made to seem so crucial. The fact that you get through the process at all is a testament to your worthiness.

I often say, "I only recommend vet school to people I don't like." I joke that you spend the same amount of time in vet school that someone does in prison for armed robbery. It's four years of hard-time until you get released on your own recognizance. The problem with vet school is that there really is no adequate description to outsiders that can convey the soul-crushing nature of those four years. I think if you had asked anyone in my class at graduation, if they would do it over again, they would probably say "yes". However, there would be a long pause and a thousand-yard stare before that answer was given. People will say, "I've heard vet school is hard to get into." I answer, "Yes, but it's even harder to get out." I look at those four years as the worst of my life. And I loved undergrad, so I had a pretty good comparison as to how things could be. I don't tell people I graduated from UCDavis. I tell them I *survived* UCDavis. I feel I became a veterinarian *despite* vet school, not because of it. The saying is "that which does not kill you makes you strong". Once you've graduated, you're strong. You're like Hulk-strong. For instance, a couple of years out of vet school I caught ebola…….kicked its ass! Just kidding. Ebola doesn't have an ass.

You'll find a lot of the advice I have to give is informed by my early experiences in school, because I see some of those same wrongs being perpetuated on associates and interns in clinical practice. Much of the way students are treated are how I hear associates and staff being treated and I reject the "management" approach of belittling and micro-managing, of setting higher and ambiguous goals while providing less and less support.

Something to understand in our run-up to being a full-fledged veterinarian: all those obstacles, and tests, and hours of studying, hours of volunteering, hours of working to reach our goal are all done when we're younger. Once we're in practice, a lot of clinic management will insist on a certain level of performance, usually a level that is not sustainable year after year. We may be up for it initially because we're excited and we've been primed to always be "on", to perpetually perform, to impress our colleagues and fellow workers. As we mature, we get friends and family and hobbies and children, yet we still have that impulse always to be doing and giving for the sake of the animals. Besides clients, some practice owners and managers take advantage of that. Just as they do with starry-eyed pre-vets, so they take advantage of associates who are just thankful for any job after school. To some degree we outgrow defining ourselves solely as a veterinarian. And we feel guilty, or are made to feel guilty, when we aren't fully occupied in doing animal care. It's been ingrained in us to say "yes" to everything. "Yes" we will do all those things to get into school. "Yes" we will do everything a professor or clinician tells us to do, no matter what. Then it becomes "Yes" to everything a boss tells us to do or a client requests/demands of us. It's ingrained behavior, like the well-worn tire grooves in a dirt road. To some degree new vets are suffering from the decades of previous generations turning clients into "customers". Are you a "customer" or a "patient" of your medical doctor? I know you see the difference. We have to decide whether we are in this profession for the short term or the long haul, because we are literally killing ourselves as caregivers. You don't have to be all things to all people at all times – because if you are doing that, you aren't being what you need to be for yourself.

There was a time when vets lacked sufficient business acumen. I understand that. There's a dichotomy of being a medical profession but also a small business and this causes mental and emotional friction. How we finesse that divide is up to each of us to figure out based on our comfort level. However, the drive to get more business savvy has led to never saying "no" to a client. I hear this from associates all the time. Business hours are until 7PM. However, if a client shows up at 6:55, even if not an emergency, they are told they still have to see them, because of the fear that the client will take their business elsewhere or give a bad review, etc. This is part of the problem and also why older practice owners are objecting to younger vets wishing to work normal, decent hours, set boundaries, and get paid properly. Practice owners need to take into consideration the morale of their staff as well, as this kind of behavior affects more than just the associate.

The pressures are different than they were twenty years ago. We shouldn't be riding the backs of new grads, expecting them to work 70 – 80 hours a week because we feel they have to "pay their dues". That's not okay. It wasn't okay when it was done to earlier generations either and yet they seem to have forgotten that. Considering the enormously higher debt load, the higher level of medicine, and the even higher level of societal expectations, what we owe those who come behind us is to find ways to make things easier for them, not harder. And if you're one of the practice owners I've heard from who are fair to their employees and understand the life/work balance, I give thanks to you.

After school, I had about $70,000 in loans (1990s economy) and the best job I could find offered $28,500, working about 50 – 60 hours a week, no benefits and only one week of vacation after the first year. Which is why I joined the Army Veterinary Corps. Better pay, benefits, a *lot* of vacation time. The Army is not for everybody. Heck, it wasn't even really for me; square peg/round hole analogy. I enjoyed my time in the Vet Corps. I got paid to exercise as part of my day. It had a lot of variability, which my undiagnosed attention-deficit disorder appreciated. My bosses were usually located hundreds of miles away from me and I was fond of saying, "What they don't know, doesn't hurt me." I had more autonomy in the Army than I would have had as an associate. Steep learning curve, however, especially with surgery, considering there wasn't anybody working with me with whom I could double-check things with or bounce ideas off. "Should that be bleeding like that?" "Why do I have parts left over after every surgery?" "Oh, my God! Why did that fall off? I didn't even touch it!" In five years, I'm proud to say that nothing died under my watch unless I intended it. It's where I also appropriated what they say about plane crashes as an analogy to surgery; any surgery you could walk away from alive was a good one. Which I also now use to define a good day. When I think back to the amount of sweating and creative use of curse-words as a first-year vet doing surgery with no training wheels, this is remarkable. Also, it's why I still detest surgery.

I'm going to talk more in the money section about how my time in the Army affected my view about clients and financial discussions.

I started drawing cartoons before vet school. I just decided to do about a dozen cartoons for a practice I'd been at as an assistant-assistant-assistant technician to encapsulate some of the funny things that had happened while I was there. They seemed to like them. Had never put pen to paper before like that. Then school provided a lot of material and drawing became a requisite as therapy. I still blame vet school for nearly killing my sense of humor. Vet school, for a time, destroyed my fundamental nature and I'll never forgive them for putting me or anyone through such misery. The irony is not lost on me that I volunteered for this torturous gauntlet, like Dante getting his personal tour. The fact that my family was subjected to the process offends me on a very deep level; I can't help but bear responsibility for that. Because I came to realize, it wasn't just me that was struggling. And oh, so unnecessarily. It's not difficult to reach out your hand to someone to give aid, but the school seemed able to only put their hand out to slap your other cheek. Cartoons helped and continue to help vent my frustrations and I hope in drawing them, as in this book, they could also help others. My cartoons are my armament; laughter my sword. I try to find humor in the absurd things that happen in a typical day. I try to soften or disarm the blow of abuses that gets directed toward us.

I have drawn over 1,500 cartoons since school, some of which you'll find in this book, some that will hopefully show up in future books. I've often felt there is a humor deficit in this profession, hypohumoria, as if it seems a little taboo if we don't take everything seriously. I love this profession and the people in it. I am irreverent, it's true. I often set myself up in disagreement with a lot of the advice that gets shoved our way particularly when I recognize advice that simply asks us to do more or to sublimate ourselves for the sake of a job. This is the antithesis of what we should be doing. You'll find I upend some long-held assumptions in this book. Anything I do, even if you may disagree with my approach, is to try to protect us as individuals as we navigate our lives and chosen career. I look to lessen the levels of stress society places upon us, even if it's subliminal. There's a lot we can't change. We can't change society's view of us or what people like to try to use against us. We can change how we react to it and try to dull the edges so we aren't cut so deeply.

I have now been in private practice as a co-owner for over twenty years. We jealously guard our hours. It is a rare event that we stay over-time. I do this for me, but also for my staff, because I recognize they have lives outside of the practice. When we're at work we will do our best when we're there. If we can find something to laugh about or enjoy each other's company as well, then great. But when our work is done, it's done. We go home. I tell clients "no" and allow my associate to do so as well. There needs to be a paradigm shift in practice. And it's going to be hard for many. Forty hours is enough to work in any job. You can still make a good living. If you want or need to do uncompensated animal work outside of the job, pace yourself. It's all about balance.

I'm a doctor!
I'm a doctor!
I'm a doctor!
Guess whaaat....?
?
DVM
New Graduate

*****

Whoa! This is so weird! Roscoe, here, makes the seventh idiopathic case today!
New Vet

"Who are you?! What have you done with Dr. Phillips!"

When new associates first meet clients

*****

New vet. Just moved. Arrived.... five minutes ago.

"How do they know?"

"I know you're just moving in, but I only have a simple question."

Anyone else find their ears to be full at the end of the day?

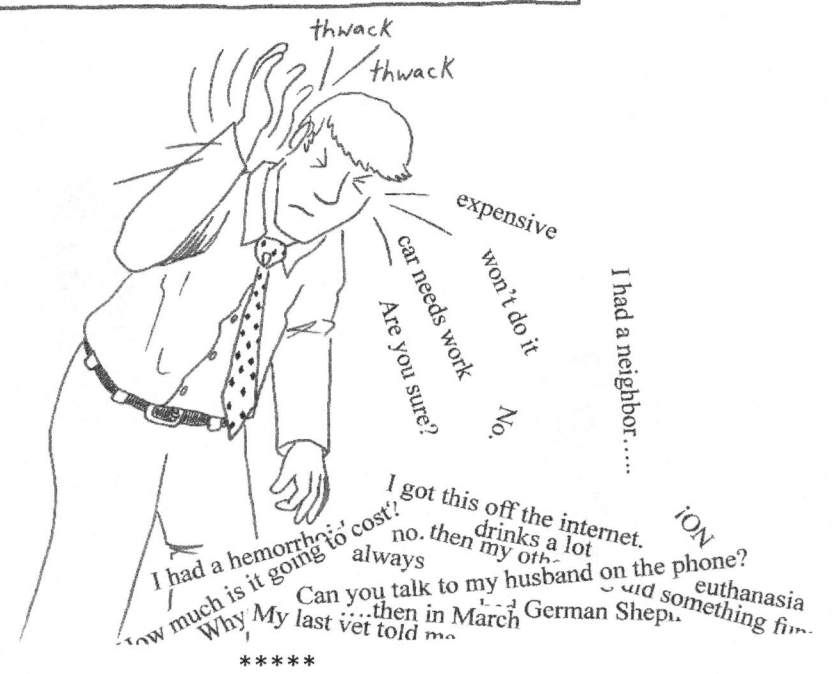

thwack thwack

expensive · won't do it · car needs work · Are you sure? · No. · I had a neighbor..... · I got this off the internet. · drinks a lot · no. then my oth... · I had a hemorrhoid · how much is it going to cost? · always · Can you talk to my husband on the phone? · euthanasia · ...said something fi... · Why · My last vet told me · ...then in March · German Shep... · ION

*****

You're our favorite doctor!*

*even though we haven't been in for four years, and go to other vets in area, and use vaccine and low-cost clinics, and complain about your prices, etc.

You think 'X' is difficult? I've been through vet school! This? This thing you're complaining about? This is nothing.

When clients balk or complain about performing simple tasks (giving ear meds, bringing in urine or feces, rechecks, etc.) I sometimes think the above

*****

Someone told me you were a vet! I thought while we're waiting out here anyway, you could help me. My dog has lupus, Cushing's, diabetes, and pneumonia. Can I tell you how my vet's treating him and you can tell me if it's ok or not?

SCHOOL BUS STOP

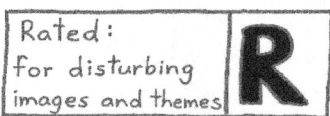

Half sane – Half vet

Clive Barker's

Curse of the Veterinarian

Hide your children! Once bitten, they are doomed to walk the earth as vets!

They thirst for blood!!

Rated: R for disturbing images and themes

*****

"So.... what do you do?"

"uh.....I'm a veterinarian."

Must. Ask. Questions.

"So, how was your day?"

"Let me put it this way. 6,799 days until retirement."

*****

Dr. Bob's last day of work before retiring

WAITING ROOM
SIT * STAY

Dear Younger and Less-Grey Me

Look at you! You're all excited having managed to navigate the veterinary education equivalent of Class 7 white-water rafting! You're heading out into the world like a squinty puppy looking for milk. You're not sure if you're even ready. Here's the thing - you're right, you're not. However, I am here from the future, to help. I just wanted to tell you some things that will hopefully make your life easier as you move forward. We'll start with some of the smaller observations and work our way up in importance.

If all of the bloodwork and other diagnostics are completely normal and the pet is still going down-hill, it's cancer. We get taught to look for growths, tumors, changes in bloodwork. More often than not, you aren't given these kinds of obvious indicators. It's a tough one because it becomes difficult to prove without pursuing ever higher diagnostics which the owner is often reluctant or unwilling to do. Doesn't mean it's not true though.

If you want to know how often a pet is bathed by an owner, you will have to ask the question twice. This is a weird human behavioral quirk. And it's just about a 100% rule. No matter how I ask the question to try to find the frequency of bathing a pet gets, the owner will answer something like, "We just bathed him Tuesday." Which obligates me (after an internal sigh) to ask the question once again, before they tell me, weekly, monthly, etc.

Make sure you go to the bathroom before doing a euthanasia. You may think I'm joking, but I'm not. You don't know if you're in for a prolonged euthanasia or not, whether due to uncooperativeness of a vein or patient, or just listening to stories, or commiserating with an owner after the fact. This becomes extremely difficult if you have a full bladder yelling at you.

People will tend to believe the first person who gets to them. Unfortunately, that probably won't be us. The internet, the breeder, the pet store clerk, the neighbor, a relative, will have given an owner their wisdom on just about every issue from diet to grooming to vaccinating to neutering. Typically, half of your conversation with owners will be about what they've been told is wrong. And they'll be very suspicious of your advice and motivations. Not much to be done about it. Just realize it.

It's important when talking with clients to recognize whether you are just addressing misinformation, a misunderstanding, or if you are up against a client's belief system. Like a person's religious outlook, if a client Believes something to be true, you will have little luck in convincing them differently. Raw diets, coconut oil, grain-free diets, the uselessness of vaccines, the toxicity of benign products are only a sampling of these types of issues. This applies to the whole spectrum of animal husbandry and care. If you recognize the True Believers soon enough, you can save yourself a lot of time, effort, and frustration. You still give them the correct information, just don't get too wrapped up in it if you find yourself metaphorically or literally banging your head against the wall.

An owner will often arrive in an exam room with a pre-diagnosis. They may even have reams of information downloaded from the interwebs, because they think in some way, we need help. As an addendum, the majority of the time the average layman's pre-diagnosis is diabetes.

PU/PD? Diabetes. Limping? Diabetes. Sneezing? Diabetes. The problem with this pre-diagnosis scenario is instead of pursuing the real problem, you have to explain why something isn't what they think it is (especially without any testing) and also having to deflect "just treating" it for the presumptive problem and "let's see what happens". And many people will be put off when you don't support their preconceived notions. Just by the law of averages, it will be diabetes some times and they will proudly take credit for the diagnosis because they "just knew it".

You know a client will be looking something up on the internet if they pull out a pen and paper and ask, "How do you spell that?" This will apply to actual or possible diagnoses and medications.

Dog food is the most over-thought issue. There are thousands of different dog foods. Everyone has their favorite. Many clients are vehement enemies of certain brands. No one seems to recognize the marketing that drives the trends of certain dog foods being "bad" and others "good", taking advantage of peoples' ignorance and prejudice. Dog food choices often fall into belief systems as spoken about above. Raw food diet people? Good luck getting them to change. Or to understand why their dog continues to have vomiting and diarrhea issues. Make a recommendation for a particular brand? You must be getting a kick-back from that company! Allergies? Must be, has to be food-related and don't tell them any different! Diseases? The internet will gladly tell a client how dog food caused it, from ear infections to neoplasia. It's even gotten to the point that before you ever see a patient with any problem, an owner will have randomly changed the brand of food to see if that would fix it. You won't have these same levels of discussion when it comes to cat food. Only dog food.

OPLD (Old Person/Little Dog) syndrome, you'll find, is a real thing. The small-breed dog will usually present with nebulous signs and the owner will be 65 years or older. Your problem here is in ascertaining whether there is an actual problem or not. Which sounds easy, but is not. Are you dealing with someone who is so attuned to their pet that they're picking up on a subtle, emergent disease process? Or are you dealing with someone's perceptions and over-reaction because they have nothing better to do but stare at their pet for any variance in their behavior, coat, or the timbre of their whine. Typically, the dog will have nothing in the way of external signs and the owner will not be forthcoming as to exactly what is wrong. And there is nothing in the 5 Minute EZ book that will guide you. Good luck, you plucky little nipper!

You're also going to find that you spend more time talking about how things are normal than any time you spend explaining treatment for diabetes or describing what Cushing's disease is. Besides OPLD, there will be many occasions owners will bring you what appear to be perfectly healthy animals. Yet, "he's never lain in that part of the yard before" will be your only clue. Or "his urine is yellow". This one even had the owners emphasize, "You don't understand! It's *really* yellow! Especially in the morning!" I wondered what the color of the urine had been, that when it turned yellow, they worried. I had another where the owner described how when they went to bed, the dog was on the couch sleeping. When the owner got up the next morning, the dog was STILL SLEEPING ON THE COUCH! All I could think was, "What if the dog had woken up first, panicked, called the owner's physician and told them the owner went to bed last night and when the dog got up in the morning he was STILL IN THE BED!" You can work up these ambiguous cases and you may be faced with clients who don't understand why everything is coming back normal. And you'll spend so much time doing a weird intellectual rumba where you have to acknowledge their concerns without dismissing them, but keep emphasizing how everything seems fine. I've had two stock answers that help. One is that we don't all run at 100% every day. Sometimes we're operating at 80%. We're not ill, just not at a 100%. The second is to lean heavily on a behavioral component. We don't perceive things the same way they do; their sense of smell is more acute than ours, for instance. If an opossum goes through the back yard at night and we aren't aware of it, but they are because of a novel smell, perhaps they freak out and act odd. They have a reason for acting strangely, we just aren't aware of it. Amazingly, these perfectly healthy animals will take up quite a bit of your time explaining all the reasons they seem fine. You will prefer these types of visits over the people who wait six months on a problem before eventually finding a convenient time in their life to bring the pet in.

You will see many surveys listing our profession as the "most trusted". Do not trust these surveys. While intellectually I believe people are telling the truth when answering such surveys, this does not translate into reality. Clients seem very unwilling to trust when faced with a medical problem that requires a financial investment. Just see the daily conversations about charges and defending your medical viewpoint against the owner's friend who was a veterinary technician several years ago.

You are going to worry over many things that never happen. You will have sleepless nights second-guessing yourself (did I clean that wound well enough? did I apply the bandages too tightly? what if my sutures slip? why didn't I think about doing an ACTH stim test?). The same brain that got you through vet school will now turn against you because you now know more than you did and are fully cognizant of all of the things that can go wrong. This is ok up to a point. Worrying makes you look things up (and you will do a great deal of this, especially in your first five years). Worrying makes you double-check things and ask colleagues' advice. Worrying is also wearying. And this is what you have to watch out for. Because even though earlier I stated that you're not ready. You are. You just have to trust yourself. You will also get better and more efficient. It may seem opaque to you now, however over time, everything will get easier. You will find that most of what you dread does not happen because you are conscientious and good at what you do. The dawn after that sleepless night will show you the right answer. You may fumble a bit. Everyone does. You learn from it and move on.

Even though vet school seemed inimical, I'm sorry to say you'll probably also end up being surprised and disappointed by your fellow Man. You thought grade school was tough? People will say meaner things to you as an adult and they won't wait until recess. Clients will lie. Clients won't listen. Client compliance will seem like a myth you can't make better with coconut oil. I'd rather you know this now than having to learn it as you go and think you're doing something wrong. It's not you. It's them. I don't know why they act the way they do and I have no answer for it other than this: it only hurts you if you believe what they say. Also, cherish those other, good clients, as rare as they might seem. I can think of some right now that do listen, that do what I ask, whose company I enjoy because we agree to collaborate on making their pet better; the ones that make this job seem effortless. Remember these people in tough times, because even if they don't tell you, they do appreciate you.

There are going to be things you just can't fix. There will be disease processes that, given anyone's best efforts, will not respond. There will be cases you can or have fixed but are constantly thwarted by the clients' actions. Don't blame yourself and don't shoulder the burden or guilt in these instances. Sometimes all you can do is mitigate a problem. Don't make it part of your job to take responsibility for things you have no control over.

You might know this already, but you are not the best, the brightest, the smartest, the most talented. And that's ok. What you do well, you do well. You're like Wolverine of the X-Men: you're the best there is at what you do. While you may look enviously upon others' skills, they can't do what you do either. You have strengths and weaknesses. Leverage your strengths, minimize your weaknesses or work on making them better. You'll find over the years that your days will be measured not by miraculous healings or grand contributions to veterinary medicine knowledge, but by the small victories. Don't lose sight of those.

The best part of your career is going to be the people you work with. You'll be constantly amazed at your support staff wherever you go. They'll be the people that make your days so much easier. They'll have those strengths that you lack and ultimately be the real reason you show up to work every day. Well, that, and the paycheck. Oh, my God, I am in it for the money!

Finally, don't be so hard on yourself. Keep second-guessing yourself to a minimum; there will be plenty of other people willing to do it for you. Those same people will try to bring you down - don't help them. To quote the words of the great sage Stuart Smalley, "You're good enough. You're smart enough. And, doggone it, people like you."

Suicide and Mental Health

Sophia Yin was a classmate of mine. She was, by all outward measures, a happy and successful person. A leader in the behavioral field. She committed suicide in 2014. I didn't know her well. We had superficial conversations over the years, mostly via email. I think we both came from the point of view of trying to help students' lives, her through her *Nerdbook*, me through humor and cartoons. I'm so sorry she is no longer with us.

When the study came out that showed veterinarians are four times as likely to commit suicide than the general population, twice the level of any other medical profession, this shocked a lot of people. Not me. Because I've seen and felt the toll this profession takes, from pre-vet, through vet school, then into our careers. I was more surprised that others were surprised by these findings. That tells me that we'd been ignoring things for a long period of time.

There was another study that showed military members are twice as likely to commit suicide than the general population. Our risk factors are actually greater than those in the military? That's astonishing. Especially since we hear so much about military suicides, probably because there is a greater population of military members than veterinarians. And society understands the military aspect better. When I think of the list of potentially most-stressful occupations, being in the military is on it. And I can't count my five years as a Veterinary Corp Captain as equal to others' military experience. Not by a long-shot. If I compare my day-to-day veterinary job with that of a soldier at a forward operating base in Afghanistan, away from their family, in hostile territory, there is no doubt that the soldier is operating under more compounded mental stress than me. So, why the disparity in suicide rates? I think the answer lies in the mental attitude prior to entering either field.

When people enter the military, there is an understanding of what they may be getting themselves into, no matter how subconscious. The training that soldiers undergo lays the groundwork for the discipline, mental and emotional buttressing needed to complete their jobs and their missions. There is also a support system in place where soldiers help each other or can seek help for mental health and emotional strain issues, though many feel more could be done. Even with all of this in place, there's still a high suicide rate.

In contrast, when people enter the veterinary field, we are flat-out not prepared for the grueling stress that the job entails. We approach the field in a very emotional way. Academia does a poor job of preparing us to deal with the public as the devouring beast that it is. School also sets the bar for how they define success so high that few can achieve it, therefore leading many to feel inadequate. All of the traits that got us to and through vet school suddenly seem like detriments. The intelligence that helped us achieve competitive grades now may lead us to doubt. We end up being someone who knows so much that we recognize the shades of gray and uncertainty in treatments and diagnoses. Yet we are faced with clients who want or demand black and white answers. The tenaciousness we used to tackle every obstacle is now either thwarted by a client who balks at procedures or a disease condition that resists treatment despite our best efforts. Our stubbornness to get things right always worked before, because they were personal goals, something we could overcome in ourselves if we just pushed harder. Before and during school we were always able to just bear down, read more, study more, and make things work. Once in practice, unfortunately, we find how little control we have over things and other people; disease processes remain obstinate and uncaring of the energy, time, and emotion we are devoting. It can be very frustrating; we feel personally responsible. Such unsurety causes us to give even more of ourselves until the phrase self-sacrifice, something usually laudatory, becomes corrupted and literal. We are fixers. We are trained to think our whole lives that everything is fixable. Vet school certainly drums that thought into our heads; I distinctly remember the implication that any negative outcome must be because of a fault within myself, some oversight or failing. As if, as long as one follows the diagnostic and/or treatment protocol, everything will be fine. It's just not true. Life and medicine are much more complicated than that.

We start questioning why we aren't getting rewarded as we used to. We start questioning our self-worth and our abilities. It doesn't help that clients pressure us with their own perceptions of our limitations. We need to remember that we are still that amazing, strong person that surmounted every obstacle to get to where we are. Very few people would have the wherewithal to do so. So many people have wanted to be veterinarians and few achieve it. Do not minimize what you've been through and how much you know. It is vastly superior to the average person. This is not ego; this is fact.

We can be our own worst enemies. I believe that those traits that comprise us are still useful and valuable, we just have to use them in a different manner. For instance, I think we are coming around to realizing that we can't do it all. We are smart enough to know our limitations and acknowledge that there are only so many hours in a day, that we can't save everything. No matter how hard you try, you can only do your best. Remember, it's *your* best I'm talking about. Not your classmates, not your colleagues. Yours. We all have strengths and weaknesses. We do ourselves a disservice when we compare ourselves to others and think we're not good enough. Because those people you're comparing yourself to? They're doing the same thing – looking at you and finding themselves wanting. No one is perfect. Some put on a better mask than others. We can always improve. But in improving, remember what you're good at. Don't discount that. There are others who can't do what you do. No one can be you. And you are good enough. I've often joked that I don't trust people who say they'll give me "110 percent". They can't. It's impossible. Even if I were to entertain it, then I have to think they're only doing 90% on something else and banking that other 10%. In other words, you cannot devote 100% of yourself to your job. It is not fair to you, to your friends and family, or even to your clients and patients ultimately. You have to be willing to let go of some things, if only for your sanity.

As an example of something we aren't adequately prepared for, something that caught me off-guard in this job, is the amount of passive neglect I witness on a daily basis. People who have the capability of making a minimal effort to greatly aid in a pet's health and they just don't do it. Nothing you could take to trial as abuse cases, just, you know, they don't take proper care of their own animal. They lapse in their care. They don't want to spend, well, *any* money. They're incomplete in giving medications. And often find the logic in blaming us for their lapses. It can weigh on your soul. It has certainly made me think less of the human race, even if there are some rare, dedicated individuals I run across that give me hope.

Returning to the comparative suicide rates between the military and veterinary fields, they have more to do with expectations and preparedness. We in the veterinary community are often caught unawares when our years of training and our earnest, honest approach in giving care to animals is met with disdain, resistance, or an uncaring eye by clients. We are given no tools or insight as to how to mitigate our stress and how that stress is compounded by the number of hours many of us work. There are few resources available and the time commitment needed to get help is, in itself, stressful. I've heard things are changing, but I think we're running way behind the curve on the problem.

We need to do a better job collectively of not necessarily "deterring" people from the field, but giving them more realistic expectations. We need to get our members to understand that they are human and, therefore, imperfect. We need to apply the motto "first, do no harm" to ourselves. Many of the client complaints I've dealt with over the years are, at their core, accusations of not being perfect. Guilty. Never said I was perfect. However, I know that realization can be difficult for some of us or we feel it is a cop-out.

A better understanding needs to be laid out as to what vets will encounter in practice. There is more attention being given to mental health programs in vet schools. This needs to carry-over into our practice years. I would recommend that a small part of CE be mandated to classes about mental health, drug abuse, depression, suicide, life-work balance. Not to add CE but to require some of CE to be devoted to the above. We already allow some CE to be business related. Seems to me to be equally, if not more, important to offer such classes. Local and state VMAs need to offer more mental health resources. I think it is important for the AVMA and its subsidiaries to offer such structure. In offering these services we remove some of the stigma of feeling like we have to deal with things ourselves or we are showing weakness by asking for help.

When I was in Taekwondo and someone heard that I did martial arts, they would get excited and ask, "Oh, wow! What belt are you?" And I'd reply, "I'm a brown belt." And the light in their eyes would fade as they said, "Oh." The unspoken reason was clear – if you weren't a black belt, it didn't count. Now, when someone finds out I'm a doctor, they eagerly ask, "Oh, wow! What kind of doctor are you?" "I'm a veterinarian." "Oh," they'll say, disappointed. (of course, that's the response from people who don't need free advice from me in the moment) It sometimes feels like we're the brown belt of the medical professions. We're not "real doctors" or as I like to retort when that comes up, "Yeah, I'm the plastic kind."

Here's what we need to remember: we're amazing! We populate the Centers for Disease Control and Prevention, the World Health Organization, the U.S. Department of Agriculture and a slew of organizations for disaster relief, food safety and inspection, public health initiatives, environmental protection, zoonotic disease identification and containment, food animal production, medical research, epidemiology and so many more!

Brown belts? I beg to differ. We're the 10th-degree black belt of the medical professions. We're the equivalent of the Swiss Army knife or the Ginsu blade, we cut through anything, even aluminum cans!

Think about how we outshine the human side of medicine within our own practices. Sure, a pet owner may wait a bit on occasion. However, we know for a fact we're going to wait a significant amount of time when we see our own physician – every time we go. And they aren't dealing with half the things we are. Your GP isn't doing a euthanasia in the next room before coming in to see you (at least I hope not). Or reviewing radiographs and blood work with a patient done the same day in the same facility. Or seeing emergency walk-ins. Or balancing hospitalized patients along with their well-visits. Our clients are much more likely to actually speak with their doctor or have the veterinarian call them about results. Clients even expect it. We don't expect that from physicians. The fact that we call clients with results instead of charging them for another office visit is another way we contrast ourselves with our medical brethren. We spend a significant amount of uncompensated time with clients on the phone. We even dispense medicine from our own practice. Can you, as a patient, get anything done at your doctor's office other than an exam? Nope.

We juggle so many disciplines (with the help of our incredible staff) that our clients, as well as ourselves, take it for granted. In a typical day we can exercise in many disciplines as a gastroenterologist, dermatologist, cardiologist, pediatrician, critical care, radiologist, orthopedist, public health expert, oncologist, behaviorist, endocrinologist, surgeon, dentist, neurologist, internal medicine, pathologist, pharmacologist, pulmonologist, anesthesiologist, OB/GYN, physical therapist, and ophthalmologist. Besides our side excursions of financial advisor, grief counselor, psychiatrist, marriage counselor, father-confessor, social worker, day-care assistant, etc. It's just expected and assumed, but it's not appreciated.

We do all this and think to ourselves this is normal every day stuff. No! Take a moment to savor how awesome you are. Take the time to acknowledge how much you do and how effortless you make it look. I think we can be too hard on ourselves. Can we always improve? Sure. But let's not lose sight of how we outdo our peers in the medical professions. The next time a client makes you think you haven't done enough for them or something hasn't gone the way you hoped, and you're beating yourself up, just remember how much you already do and give yourself some credit. You. Are. Awesome!

This may come across as egotistical to you. You may even feel yourself resisting this viewpoint, feeling yourself not worthy. But it's one of the reasons I don't accept a lot of the criticism that comes our way. Because I know you. You hard-working, honest, earnest people doing your best out there! And it upsets me what we have to deal with beyond just the usual struggles of the job, when everyone else's perceptions are that in some manner they could do better. They think they have a say in how we do things or who we are. And they don't. They don't understand at all. It's not to say I'm the best and smartest person on the planet, but when it comes to being a veterinarian, yes, I certainly know better than the average client coming in for help. Don't give us crap about it and make our lives more difficult! I don't know anything about cars. I'm hopeless when it comes to doing anything handy or using power tools. Other people are good at those things. I rely on them to do their best and do a good job. I don't belittle their efforts. I don't question everything they do. I don't yell at them. Even if things go awry or not as expected, I trust them enough to assume they're doing their best and, hey, look, sometimes things are more difficult than they first appeared and unexpected things happen. Frustrating? Yep. But not to the point I'm going to abuse someone as so often happens to us.

I heard this analogy (paraphrased here) was said by President Kennedy in reference to journalists who critiqued his every move: "There was a baseball player who hit a home run every time he was up at bat. When in the field, he caught every ball that came his way. He ran faster, hit harder and more accurately than anyone else. His every move and decision was perfectly made. Now, if only he'd get off the couch and actually play….." And so it is with clients. I ask anyone who has been in the profession more than three days, what word follows each of these sentences:

"I don't want to offend you…."

"I'm not a veterinarian…."

"I don't want to bad-mouth the last vet I saw…."

You know the answer without me telling you. And feel free if someone ever starts to use the second example on you, hold up your hand and say, "That is a complete sentence."

Clients aren't the only one who think they can do our job better than us. Pretty much everyone thinks they have a say – the groomer, the breeder, the neighbor, the trainer, pretty much anyone with a tongue or can do sign-language. And it won't just be medical things of which they will share their unsolicited opinions. It'll be the way you run your practice, your hours, your staff, your body language, the perceived smells in your practice, the décor, your written prescription policies, the practice location, your recall policies, oh please, it's really an endless list. I know I'm repeating myself when I say this, but it only matters what you feel comfortable doing. The first five years of practice I took this type of unsolicited advice to heart and tried to change my tone, my language, how much or how little I explained, trying to match things or do things better with each subsequent client. Five years later, still getting complaints, still getting lay-splained how to do things better. Yeah, do things better for that particular individual at that particular time for that particular circumstance. There is absolutely no way to continue this. So, I stopped. Today, clients get the person they're going to get. Like me. Don't like me. Don't care. Of course, I care, just not to the point that I'm going to cancel my basic nature to please someone in the moment. Because there'll be someone else coming right around the corner wanting something else done the way that pleases them best.

(As an aside, lay-splained is my term for layman trying to explain things to us. In case that term threw you. I made it up. I make up a lot of things.)

Our lives have been all-animals, all the time. If you're among those that has found this profession to not be as fulfilling as you thought it would, try to find something outside of it that gives you energy. This is a multi-faceted piece of advice. First, acknowledge that it is ok to view what has been your passion and your goal of many years as a job. I think few people, no matter how optimistic, would say they find completeness and self-identity solely through their job, any job. Second, you're automatically going to have to set time aside to take care of yourself, however you choose to do so. Which means you're going to have to say "no" to a job that you've only said "yes" to up to this point. That rescue group you've been helping might get a bit irate with being told "no". Reducing your hours at work may inconvenience clients who are used to you always being available. Too bad. You need to put yourself first. Let's face it, you probably haven't been. People are great at shaming us into doing more. Heck, we're great at doing it to ourselves.

And if "no" is a difficult thing for you, practice. My spouse has a very difficult time saying "no". They're not quick enough to come up with an excuse as to why they can't and don't feel comfortable just saying they won't. You have no obligation to explain why you're telling someone "no" to something. My go-to is "I have a prior commitment" or "I have a family obligation that day". Certainly, feel free to come up with your own version. And if "no" doesn't work for you, might I offer you to try "nein", "nej", "non", "nie", or "hapana".

One of the very consistent things I've seen when I read about a veterinarian who has committed suicide is how much they were doing for and in their community. It's exhausting to read their list of accomplishments – adoption fairs, rescue group work, shot clinics, helping the homeless and their pets, the list is extensive. These high-end achievers have even made me question whether I'm doing enough. I eventually answer "yes", however their list of accomplishments is daunting and can make anyone else's seem trivial in comparison. I wonder if, when they're expending so much time and energy into one aspect of their lives, what other areas might have been suffering from neglect? I am not suggesting they brought things down on themselves. We can all just be so narrowly focused on appeasing one request after another, that we forget our own needs. And then read the praise from people for this *self-less*, giving person and how much they'll be missed. And it pisses me off! Because I'm thinking, "How many of these people praising this vet after their death, praised them in life? How many of these people asked more and more of them and took and took until the vet had nothing left to give? How many of these people directly caused the despair and emotional drain that caused the veterinarian to take their life?" If you find your job is that one area of your life that is sufficient and sustaining and makes you happy, then by all means continue! I am truly happy it does that for you. I simply worry that there are many of us out there who are letting things in our life slide while trying to live up to this idealized version of being a veterinarian. Trying to project an image either thrust upon us by others or felt necessary by our own internal motivations.

Ultimately, these clients are not considering us as a person, but as a resource. And that resource is limited. Save some for yourself. Say "no" more often. Set boundaries early. Don't allow your boss to guilt or badger you into doing more than you already do. Bosses, stop being so unreasonably demanding and disparaging to your associates and staff. Take into account not just the Average Client Transactions or number of patients seen each day, but the feelings and motivations in your staffs' lives. I understand the focus on tangible numbers, but we can't do it at the expense of the intangible and relationships that form success. You can't please everyone all the time. It is impossible. You're going to have upset people. Some clients approach life antagonistically; it's their default. Doesn't mean you have to accept it or run around scared of them. People can be unfair and manipulative. They'll try to make you feel bad for their situation, make you feel responsible for them. You are not. They are responsible for their decisions. If you choose to help people, make sure you don't do it out of guilt or pressure. Do it because *you* choose to. And do it sparingly so you don't wear yourself out. I look at things that are asked of me and ask myself, "Is this something I'd feel comfortable doing for everyone else?" In other words, if I do something for one person, I feel obligated to do it for others. For instance, I've been asked to do home-euthanasia. Would I do that for everyone? Nope. Therefore, I don't do it at all. And you'll find there are few situations that you'll do for everyone. This approach has been self-protective for me. Do I fall into doubt at times that I may be viewed as an asshole? Yeah. But, I get over it. Maybe because I am an asshole. Hard to say. But I've seen the other side of the track – the over-doing. And I know where that leads. Again, this advice may not suit your temperament. I understand. Like some practitioners say about certain medical protocols, "In my hands, this works."

It's been argued to me that that's all well and good, but there's an animal involved in these decisions. An animal that we can help. That makes saying "no" to demands difficult if not impossible. Perhaps we shouldn't be so obstinate and should be more caring and giving and understanding toward a client so that we can help that animal. And I agree. I've also found, however, that our compassion gets used against us. It's a fine line. It's a line we all have to walk every day. There will be times you give in and donate your time, energy, and own finances. You will have to set a limit to how often you can do that, because <u>everyone</u> will ask it of you, regardless of their ability to pay or follow-thru. There are times that we simply aren't going to be able to help an animal either due to restrictions of time, money, or a client's resistance. We're going to feel bad about that. I'd just like you to give yourself a break in these fraught moments. The client chose to have a pet. You did not go over to their house and force it on them. They have a responsibility toward that biological, feeling organism. If they abdicate that responsibility, it is not like a relay race where you are obligated to pick up that baton.

Should you do something you normally wouldn't for someone, make it clear that it's a one-time offer; that it won't be something you do in perpetuity moving forward. Too often you'll hear a client say, "You did it for me before!" It's ok to respond, as I have, "That may be, but I'm not doing it again" or "this time" or, in some instances, "We shouldn't have done it that way in the first place, so we're not going to compound the error by doing it again."

It was pointed out to me that when you get a group of veterinarians or veterinary technicians together an undeclared game of one-upmanship starts as to who works the hardest. We just start talking about what we do: how many hours we work, whether nights and weekends are involved, how many days in a row we work, how we incorporate our family into working pet adoptions shows, what rescue groups we work with, etc. And I think we do this, in part, because we have a worry of how we are viewed or judged, not only by society but by our peers. We want to be viewed as the good guys. We seem to think that the more we do for others, especially when we're not compensated for it, the more the world will like us. This causes many of us to over-extend. I watch the pre-vets already doing this with how many volunteer hours they've logged, already putting pressure on themselves and their contemporaries to do more. There's only so much one person can do. As has been said before, we can't fix everything. It's a bit of a marathon – pace yourself.

Someone asked me if I were a career half-full or a career half-empty kind of person. I replied I'm a career-on-fumes-oh-look-the-light-just-came-on-the-dashboard kind of person. I kid. Slightly. I'm more of a glass half-empty, but it can be refilled kind of person. I've been in conversations with the ultra-positive people in our profession and, Buddha bless 'em, they mean well. And they have a great outlook; one I wish I could emulate, but their advice is exhausting to me. Perhaps it's because I'm an introvert, I don't know. I'm happy for them because they're so earnestly positive and thriving in their jobs. A lot of their advice seems to fall under the umbrella of "if something isn't right, just change it". "Just change your attitude. Just change your perception. Just change your job!", they say. I agree with that, but it's limiting. There are things that can't be changed – death of a patient and the recrimination fall-out. There are things that can be changed but then cause enormous strife – leaving a toxic job.

For example, I had a client with a dog with chronic skin and ear issues, who would initially do the proper treatments. The dog would look fantastic! Then he'd stop treating, even though advised long-term maintenance would be needed. Six months later he'd bring the dog in looking tragic and he'd be bemoaning, "He looked so good, Doc! But look at him now!" And I'd have to have the same conversation with him and no amount of call-backs or free rechecks (he wouldn't schedule anyway) or even making it as easy as possible to simply refill the medications changed this debacle. This dog was partially treated by his owner all through his life up until euthanasia and so much of that life was spent being miserable. Frustrating? Oh, yeah. Made me want to beat that client senseless. Except I thought he already lacked enough sense. Perhaps I should have tried to knock some into him but I'm not sure which orifice I'd have used to smack it in. Here was something I could not change, no matter how much time or personal angst I invested. You just feel so bad for the pet. And these are the things that wear on us daily.

One viewpoint I take to life is this: "If there's something you can change, then you don't have to worry. Just go ahead and change it. If there's something you can't change, well, then, don't worry about that either. Because you can't change it. Which leaves not much else to worry about." And as I'll always be honest with you, I am not 100% good about following my own advice. It's a bit like a mantra. I have to trot it out to remind me and mentally buffer myself from the daily road-wear. Obviously, I remember the above dog and always will. However, this is the kind of passive neglect you'll see every day, several times a day, and have very little control of because the other supposed adult(s) in the equation aren't doing their part. The main fault I see in the everything-positive act is it lacks nuance and is rigidly absolute that change is possible, doable, even easy! Yet change isn't easy for a lot of people. And I find that it puts additional pressure on those of us where this outlook does not come naturally.

It reminds me of my visits to the hardware store. I often don't know what it is I'm asking for when I'm forced to fix something around the house. No one there should assume I have even a modicum of knowledge in the art of tools. I don't. When I talk with them, I feel like Koko the gorilla trying to convey quantum physics through sign language. No matter what project, large or small, they always tell me, "It's easy!" It's not. It's going to take me three more trips to finish the project. I'll try to avoid the people I asked questions of earlier in the day, buy the wrong size thingy, re-read the poorly written instructions and be able to teach a course on creative cursing. And it will take me four times as long as someone who knows what they're doing.

Which is a long way around to saying, I appreciate positivity, but when you tell people that change is easy, you're really saying it's easy for you. Don't presume it's that way for everyone. Doing so ignores the coping mechanisms that are just barely getting some people by every day. Presuming change is easy ignores the reality that our profession is plagued by mental and emotional health issues. Not everyone has the same intellectual and psychological tools and there are those that feel they've misplaced their toolbox altogether. The people need understanding and support, not soundbite panaceas.

When our colleagues share their feelings of hopelessness and their stories of abusive clients, unreasonable bosses, and negative internet reviews, we need to recognize that if we tell them that they just need to look at those situations differently, we're not being helpful. In fact, we may be causing harm. Those pat answers can make people feel the problem is their fault, and if they'd just fix their perceptions, fix themselves, everything would be fine. That can add to the weight of what they're already enduring.

I appreciate the positive people in our profession. I find their approach admirable. I also recognize the strain it puts on a number of us who feel inadequate in the face of their unflagging, unwavering affirmations. Our advice magazines about client complaints and insurance claim stories are also rife with how we should have done better. Not "could have done" better, but "should have". We're told to do "mirroring" techniques, know the client's Meyers-Briggs personality type, use body language, tone, eye contact, no eye contact, touching, no touching, phrasing, the use of silence, etc. All very useful advice if we live retrospectively. All communication is perfect in hind-sight; some might even say 20/20. I resent these side-line commentators. They reinforce that the onus of all interactions is on us, completely ignoring the client part of the equation.

Positivity can be a bit blind to the negative. The thinking goes, if you plow through life positively, good things happen. Yet often extremely positive people are just blessed with the ability to ignore the negative; this can be to their detriment as adverse situations or feelings are allowed to build until they overflow the banks. I think we need to acknowledge and address the negative things to fix them, if possible. Don't compare yourself with others. Don't look at that positive person over there who seems to have it all worked out and feel defeated that you can't be that way. They don't have it all worked out. They have their worries and scars. Trust me. And perhaps, if they do have it worked out, figured out that balance, they went through a lot to get there and they still struggle. And they may be the ones sharing what has worked for them. I get that. But you don't have to be them; borrow from them what works for you.

We put too much pressure on ourselves to be perfect, to be up, to be "on" all the time. To be positive in the face of anything thrown at us, whether it's client misunderstanding, abusive behavior, dealing with euthanasias, or staff interactions. We're told to give clients an "experience", a new term that's making the rounds that I've learned to loath. I don't even know what that means or how to even start addressing it. I have always done my best for each and every client and patient and will continue to do so. What is this nebulous "experience" that I am now supposed to provide? Are we now Disneyland? We're told, *go on Twitter, Facebook, have a blog*! I only see the ways that can backfire on me, which I have seen happen to others. Opening my life up more is not how I'm built. *Put up positive pictures of you and your staff playing with puppies and kittens!* I get the wonderful vibe being aimed for here. However, I don't want my face on anyone's screen and I really don't want to perpetuate the stereotype that all we do all day is play with puppies and kittens. *Go, go, go! Do, do, do! Reach out to the community! Help rescue groups! Do spay days!* If you do these and find them fulfilling, I'm happy for you. I'm not meaning to belittle anyone's accomplishments of values here. It's just these vertiginous levels of performance we're supposed to achieve, being pushed by colleagues, society, advice magazines, ourselves, just don't seem sustainable. Granted, again, I'm speaking as an introvert here. Set boundaries. Learn to say no. Know your limits.

While we are all trying to smile and be positive, we're not dealing with the deep-seated pressures working against us. We only bring things up in a corrective fashion, then return to shunting aside or minimizing the stress we're experiencing daily. Ever been yelled at by a client? Ever had to address a completely irrational request or demand and then deal with the scorched earth anger when you can't meet their needs? Ever had to shift, and strip, mental, emotional, spiritual gears when going from a euthanasia in one room to a new puppy in the next? Ever had to take the abuse a client heaps on you for a negative outcome, in the face of having done everything you could and the result probably would have been the same in anybody's hands? These are the things we don't talk about while we're all trying to be positive and uplifting. We need to acknowledge this darker side of our profession or it just festers.

We can't control everything. We are simply human. We have frailties and foibles. We also have a finite amount of ourselves to offer to the world. If you find the upbeat message works for you, I am pleased for you. If, like me, you find it limiting or ineffectual, there's nothing wrong with you. Positivity and outgoingness is natural for some people. It is not a requirement for you to be and act like them to be successful in your life. People gravitate to positiveness. I get that. Personally, I'm worn out at the end of the day interacting with people. Not burnt-out, just worn out. The last thing I need is for someone trying to pump me up and enforce some cheerfulness when all I want to do is triple-lock the door, plug in, and decompress. Just so I can drag myself back onto that hamster wheel tomorrow.

We're told to manage the expectations of our clients, yet we often don't manage our own expectations. I was recently told that all suffering comes from expectations, so to not have problems, one shouldn't have expectations. Again, a bit too absolute for me. Good for you if you can achieve this. I think you need expectations if you want to change things. I think this profession can be better for us. I have an expectation that can happen. This takes more effort than just throwing positive thoughts out into the world. It takes work. And time.

I'm not advocating wallowing in the negative. That opposite end of the spectrum can be just as unhelpful. Rather, it takes a combination of approaches and finding the tools that work for you. You can borrow tools from your neighbor. You can create approaches to problems that work for you. You may be envious of those who make it look easy, but even though it may take you more effort, or time, or more trips to the store, I think we all have the ability to work it out, even if it's not exactly the way we expected it would. Of that I am positive.

Psychologists differentiate between sympathy, empathy, and compassion. Sympathy is a feeling of care and concern for someone. Empathy is sharing in the emotions of someone else. Compassion is defined as suffering with someone else, a more engaged form of empathy, where we wish to alleviate the suffering of another.

My technician was righteously angry after presenting an estimate to a client who declared they had no intention of proceeding further, which came as no surprise to me. She was expressing compassion for the pet. That's a good thing. It's what drives us into this profession and motivates us to excel. It can, unfortunately, also be associated with guilt or frustration if our efforts to relieve suffering are thwarted. So many veterinarians end up with compassion fatigue because we approach every case, every day this way. This gets back to expectations. I strive to not have expectations of others. I wish to be pleasantly surprised when they actually do agree to things I've advised. Sometimes they fool me, do a fake-out, and I get the spiritual equivalent of a "wedgie" and I have to chastise myself with that proverb, "Fool me once, shame on you. Fool me twice, shame on me." You can't care about the pet more than the owner. Compassion expends a lot of energy when we're arguing or trying to persuade owners to help us alleviate suffering in their pets. You'd think they'd be in the same motivated position as us, if not more so, but so often are not. We blame ourselves and act as if our lack of persistence is the only reason an owner declines diagnostics or treatment. We tell ourselves we didn't do a good enough job. That isn't true, but it's how we're wired. Empathy, the down-gear of compassion, with either the owners or pets or both, can also be emotionally exhausting in a long-running career.

After a difficult surgery, I was worried because the owners weren't compliant with at-home instructions by even the most liberal of definitions. I lost sleep over this dog. I felt bad about the impact that a wider incision was going to have on the dog's recovery and the potential for bruising. I fretted over whether I sutured and ligated adequately. Even in trying to distance myself and intellectualize the surgery and after-care of what I can and can't control, my brain wanted to offer up all sorts of pessimistic scenarios. In this profession our broad knowledge can sometimes be a detriment because we know exactly how badly things can go even when we've done everything right. Bottom line, the dog was fine. This situation reminded me how I used to fret at that same sleepless level over every surgery I did in my first five years out of school.

Getting back to my technician, I found it sweet how much she showed she cared. I felt a bit bad because I resist getting to that level. I do care when a client declines to tend to their pet's needs; I care deeply. I just don't let it hurt me like it used to. I think it's important to recognize you are not less of a person, or less of a veterinarian, because you're dispassionate in the moment. In fact, this may be helpful in making rational and impartial decisions. We can still express sympathy toward a situation or plight without allowing it to scar our psyche. It's a bit like applying a layer of intellectual lidocaine over the nerves that get exposed to the abrasiveness of life. I think decoupling your emotions from a client's decision-making about pursuing diagnostics and/or treatment is a protective mechanism. Continue to advocate for the animal, but it is not a failure on our part for someone else to make bad choices.

If I could wish something for anyone entering the profession, it would be to have a shorter learning curve when it comes to easing these strong emotions. It's tough because that's how we've learned to engage in the world, and it's often how we've been rewarded by others who see that compassion in us. Our pursuit of this job has always been primarily an emotional one. That same emotion requires energy, which is a finite resource that has to feed us on many levels of life, not just our job. We have to use it wisely. We also can't let others take advantage of our compassion, diverting our energies for their selfish ends. I think this profession is like a relationship where you start off with this strong passion that flares like a newly lit match. Over time this flame becomes tempered and matures into a deeper, even more meaningful emotion. It becomes something that sustains us without burning us out.

I complain about my job. Everyone complains about their job, whether a veterinarian or not. There's a bit of a stigma about doing so with us, however. We feel we're being ungrateful or we should be more positive about having achieved our goal when so many others couldn't. While I assiduously avoid the subject, if forced, I tell people I consider what I do as just a job. I see how put-off they are by the statement and they're confounded why I don't wax on eloquently about the virtues of my calling. It's frowned upon to break the unspoken rule of not complaining about being a veterinarian. In complaining, very often it is directed at the human factor, and it feels a little like biting the hand that feeds us. I would posit that it is perfectly fine to complain about your job and this profession. I give you permission. And I have the self-appointed authority to do so. It doesn't necessarily mean you want or should leave your job or that you should feel bad that you're not as enamored with it as a fellow colleague. To complain about legitimate frustrations is a relief valve for many of us. It's also a chance to show we're in the same boat and demonstrate an understanding of what we're all going through that no one outside the profession can.

If we find being a veterinarian does not define us entirely, that's ok. You're not less of a veterinarian for wanting more outside the job, more out of life. I am thrilled when I don't have to work. Honestly, when I leave this profession, I will not be looking with fondness at it in my rearview mirror. I will lie to the other denizens of the worn-down people's home my kids will choose for me when asked what I used to do for a living. I've decided my answer will be "arboreal census taker". And if they inquire further I'll clarify, "I counted trees." Just because I don't invest even more of myself than I currently do is a choice. While I haven't forgotten why I got into this job, I also have to conclude that this is not the job I thought it would be.

I'm pretty proud of coining the phrase "idiot fatigue". Because I think many of us don't suffer from compassion fatigue, but rather more from exposure to the crass, uncaring, demanding entity we call "the public". I've also heard the word "ethics fatigue" and "moral fatigue" and I have to admit I start feeling a bit amused that even here we feel the need to define our fatigue in some manner. I think it's quite enough to say we're drained without delineating between ennui and debility. Ethics fatigue, as I understand it, is being thwarted in our attempts to help. I don't care for this definition because it's the lack of ethics or general care-taking on the part of the client, not the veterinarian. Ethics fatigue makes it sound like it's the vet that is being unethical in their approach and I don't care for things that imply that we are at fault in some manner when we're not. I, and you, are not responsible for the decisions that clients make. Advocating for animals to people who don't follow or appreciate our advice is a serious stressor. That's why you have to divorce yourself from that stressor to some degree. The burden of the decision to not treat is on the owner, not us. It is not a failure on our part for someone else to make choices inimical to their pet. Is this exhausting? Yes. Is it frustrating? Oh, yeah. I think we suffer from the realization that many pet owners are not as invested in their pets as we thought when considering this profession. It can be very disheartening. But, it's also why I think idiot fatigue is a better term, even if it may seem crass and too broad-sweeping for some people's sensibilities.

I wish I had the answers for the succubus of depression that so many people have to deal with. To say this profession is difficult is like saying brain surgery on a battlefield is difficult. I hope many of you are reaping the rewards of being a veterinarian. If, however, that is not the case, find outlets away from the job. I do many non-vet, non-animal related things. I have to in order to give my psyche a break.

I go to work, do a good job, and then leave work. I don't do extra-curricular animal-related activities. I don't do "spay days". I don't help rescue groups. I don't volunteer my time at shelters or the like. If you do, you will never hear me judge. I used to help out a couple of rescue groups. I used to do free spays and neuters through a county voucher program. I discovered that not only isn't it appreciated, there were constant demands for me to do more and more for less and less; though I'm not sure what less than free is, many of these "clients" were determined to find out. The amount of complaints and anger I and my staff received from people for free services was unexpected to say the least. I got off that S&M merry-go-round pretty quick. If you also don't do these things, don't kick yourself that you should be and don't let others hook you into doing so. It's ok to not do more. Speaking only for myself, my job tires me enough as it is. People exhaust me. I can't imagine doing more, without damaging myself. I'm not always perfect in keeping tendrils of work from following me home in my reptilian brain-stem. Recognize and give yourself credit that as long as you do your best, that's all that should be expected of any of us. Take care of yourselves. Take care of each other.

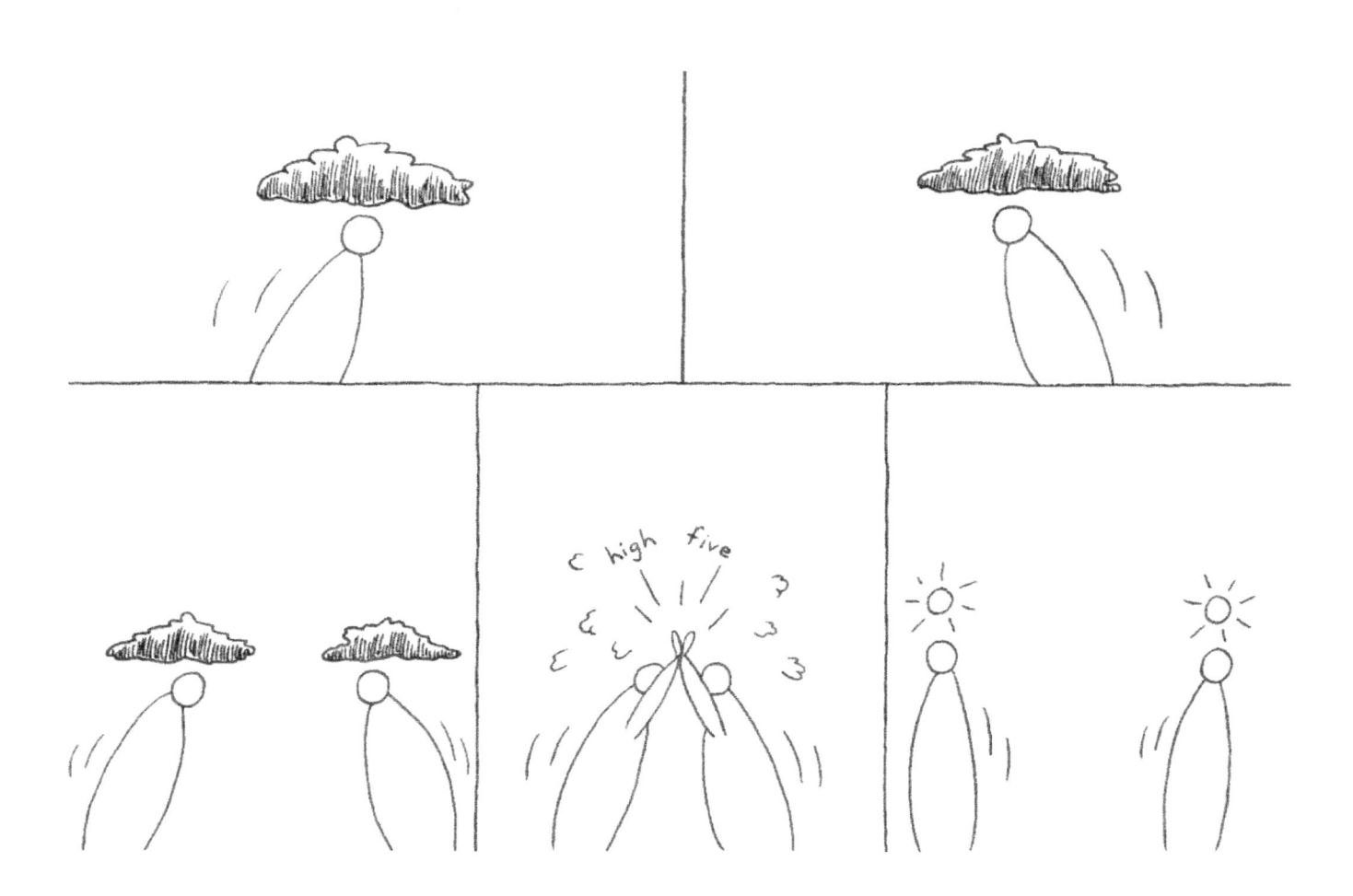

*****

38

Panel 1: PSYCHIATRIC HELP 5¢ / THE DOCTOR IS IN / "VETERINARY MEDICINE IS HARD."

Panel 2: PSYCHIATRIC HELP 5¢ / THE DOCTOR IS IN / "YOU'RE A VETERINARIAN?"

Panel 3: PSYCHIATRIC HELP $1.00 / THE DOCTOR IS IN / "PLEASE CONTINUE."

Thanks Sparky!

*****

"I'm not going to do any of that. He's just a dog and honestly, Doc, he's just not worth it."

"Dr. Scott, what are we to do with you? This is your third time in this court for assault."

"Goats!"

"Horses!"

"Ugh. People."

Future Veterinarian

*****

C'mon, Doc! Get back out there! Get on your feet! You're gonna eat lightning and you're gonna crap thunder!

Every one needs a Burgess Meredith in their practice

Are you okay?
i'm exhausted
...but fulfilled!

*****

positive thinking
thinking positive
pos-i-tive thinking
positive thinking
positive thinking
thinking
positive
positive
thinking
positive thinking
thinking positive
positive
positive
positive
positive
positive
.....and then we open the doors
Why didn't you open sooner?!
These meds didn't work!
I need!
Why haven't I been seen yet?!
I just have a quick question!
I have an emergency nail trim!
I want!
sigh

Even after establishing Fear Free ™©® protocols, Dr. Scott was still afraid of going to work

Nervous breakdown. Seems Dr. Johnson took someone's advice about giving clients his phone number and email address. To his credit, he lasted eight days.

*****

Now serving number twenty-seven! Number twenty-seven?!

YELL AT THE DOCTOR
027

*****

He starts shaking as soon as we enter the parking lot.

I know the feeling.

New Year's Resolution: don't talk negatively; only talk about the good things that happened at work
Waaaaiit. Lunch! Lunch was good!

*****

We have an emergency!
We were closing but if you can come right now we'll wait.
He's been like this for three months so we thought we should have him seen.
Must. Resist. Homicidal. Urges.

Do everything you can! My credit limit is $25,000!
Hey! A diagnosis on the first test!
All the animals are nice today!
Thank you, Dr., for everything you do!
poof
Well, that was too good to last.
beep beep beep beep

*****

Faking it all day wears me out.
IN BOX

Dr. Alexander and the Terrible, Horrible, No Good, Very Bad Day

*****

Poor Dr. Neeson. Worst case of burn-out I've ever seen!

48

Clients

Better people than me have said we need to understand problematic clients and where they're coming from; that they've been hurt and that's why they turn around and hurt others, yell at us, lash out at our staff. I disagree. I don't need to understand why a dog tries to bite me to know to muzzle it. I also disagree that there aren't people who are just sheer assholes. You go back to kindergarten and you'll find them cutting in line and stealing other children's crayons, throwing a tantrum when they don't get their way. I have no time, energy, or training to figure out which flawed human being is which. I treat everyone equally. I treat everyone as an adult. I try to do my best every day. I do my part to convey to the best of my ability what needs to happen. Have a yelling client upset at some small, often perceived, infraction? If I and my staff have done our best, this client is not going to get the response they think. I don't yell back. I don't return kind for kind. But neither do I roll over and pee on myself.

There's one story I'd like to share about treating people like adults. I had one client with some definite emotional and mental health issues. We accounted for that in our dealings with her. We often approached her gingerly like you would a child. Years go by, all is well. Until we reached a situation that we had to tell her "no" about something. No amount of insistence on her part and no amount of careful explanation on our part was going to change that. She left our practice. One parting shot was she felt insulted because she thought that we were treating her like a child. I so wanted to tell her, well, no, actually this is the first time we've treated you like an adult and that's what's really bothering you.

People are weird. And I recognize I, too, am a people, therefore I accept I am weird in my own way (please, not necessary to point out how many ways, thank you). However, I routinely feel out of sync with my fellow Earth-sharing troop. They seem like a different species. Homo clientensus, perhaps, or Homo ignoramus. I had an owner who makes a very decent living and seems in the many ways society expects, to be educated and "normal". He uses Palmolive for flea control and a "concoction" (his words) for cleaning ears that includes, in part, pink eye medication, athlete's foot powder, and salt water. He also stated that the dog is an outdoor dog except in the winter (because, you know, winters in the southern states can be pretty brutal). I told him that Palmolive is not an effective flea control. He retorted with how it was a vet who told him to do it. This is a defense many owners will bring out when you're correcting them on something. I just tell them, "I don't know what you were told elsewhere, but XYZ is not a good idea." When I told him to not use that "concoction" in the ears, he replied, "Well, it works." Granted, at the visit, the ears looked fine, but he had already said that they are a recurrent problem and he has to treat monthly, which makes it seem, that, oh, I don't know, his "concoction" doesn't work. His next line of defense against a reasonable conversation was that it cost him $500 - $600 the one time he took the dog to a vet for an ear infection, which has to be an exaggeration, because he either had other things done as well as dealing with the ear problem or he's just pulling numbers out of a bodily orifice.

Three things I took away from this conversation. One is that people aren't necessarily coming to us to get good and proper information. It's not like I'm the neighbor giving unsolicited advice. They bring their pets to us. We're going to do our job well and tell them what's best. I'm sure human physicians get ignored by their patients as well. Two, this encounter was a great example to show that ignorance crosses all educational and socioeconomic levels. The last thing is that many of us got into this profession because we are most certainly attuned more to animals than people. Yet, we can't get to the animals except through people and only if they really allow us to. They're kind of like the large bouncer determining whether to let you into the dance club or not. And the more we deal with people, the more we like the animals. It's quite a conundrum.

I've thought it odd that with all of our animal behavior experience, we don't turn that same spotlight on our fellow primates. Because they're often showing us behaviors that have rewarded them in the past or in other situations. If they're at an 11 because of a 1 or 2 level speed-bump on the road of life, they've learned that an angry display behavior gets them something – attention, discounts, free stuff, or even just the feeling of superiority over the person they're yelling at. What is happening in front of you is like the chimpanzee who has grabbed palm fronds and is flinging them around trying to seem bigger and more threatening than they are. When I confront people like this, I get calmer. Then I watch them ratchet their behavior up, trying to get a rise out of me. Which secretly amuses me, though they are unaware. They're trying to get me into the same emotional state as they're acting out, get me yelling back. I don't fall for this. And neither should you. If you return their behavior in kind, they reverse cause and effect, telling the story of how rude you were and that's what they were angry about regardless of how it started. If you give in to this behavior and accede to their demands, you are only setting yourself up for future drama with this client.

Obviously, if you or your staff have dropped the ball, then try to fix the problem. I'm not saying there won't be legitimate complaints. It's just, with those, you fix them. Move on. Granted, some people won't accept your fix and will demand more. You'll have to weigh those scenarios individually. If you've offered what you feel is a fair fix and they don't accept it, that's on them. I am saying, though, that I've found most onerous encounters with clients are part of a negotiation tactic on their part. When people say, "I'm never coming back here!" I find it very revealing when I say, "Ok" and watch them get surprised because that's not what they expected as a response. What they were expecting is for us to offer up things to them so that they don't go elsewhere, because that's what's happened at other places they've done this. Psshaw! They're an adult. "Go find a place you'll be happy! I'm rooting for you!" I also doubt there is such a place, because they'll be the same demanding and unpleasant person wherever they go.

I tend to remove myself one step when dealing with angry people. I find it helps. I disengage my emotional response (as best as possible) and observe. One thing I've observed is where people give themselves away. They do what I call "yelling at the umpire". You ever see a manager of a baseball team yelling at the umpire? They're waving their hands and kicking dirt at the ump. Few times do they get any satisfaction, but they do it any way. A client will start with a complaint about a singular issue. Whether you do or don't believe the issue is valid or do or don't offer concessions, watch the people who start waving their hands and yelling more. They start bringing up extraneous things, start grasping at other perceived slights, sometimes going back years (I'm not kidding, this has happened). They don't like your tone, the receptionist "made a face" at them, the technician's body language was rude, etc. They're metaphorically kicking dirt, trying to shore up or add to their story. It also reveals to me that they know their original complaint was probably illegitimate or they think they can take their complaint further and get more concessions by adding to it. I stick to only their initial complaint. I ignore the things they add. As I told one person, "I can't do anything about what happened three years ago. I wish you'd brought it up at the time and then I may have been able to fix it." Here's the thing – I don't believe them anyway about the incident from three years ago. Because they're showing me right now how they react to things, so why wouldn't they have done so three years before? People wear me out.

I've also dealt with people who go to 11 in their response and I've seen it cross their eyes when they realize that they're on the wrong side of things. But they've yelled themselves into a corner and they won't back down. They're also the ones that start "yelling at the umpire". I stick to the facts and the linear timeline of events and don't let emotion rule the exchange. It still impacts you when these things happen, no doubt. I just add padding by stepping back emotionally and analyzing what the client is attempting to do. I also know my internal compass of fairness works pretty well, so if I've done my best toward resolving an issue with someone and they still express dissatisfaction, that's on them. Therefore, I suppose you just have to have faith, trust, and confidence in yourself and reject a client's attempt to malign your integrity.

It's one of the things we find ourselves ill-prepared for when entering practice. We get beat up on a daily basis. We're like the pinata of the medical professions. There's the negotiation of money, of time, of conveniences, of perceptions, of needs in every client interaction. It's exhausting. People accuse us of the worst of things. Not caring. Being in it for the money. Forcing them to do something. Explaining too much. Explaining too little. Rushing them. Not hurrying enough to attend to them. And they think they're the only people who need something at that moment. We don't get enough credit in being able to manage and juggle all of these personalities and still accomplish so much good. I reject the characterization that others try to put on me. I don't have to prove my caring. I don't have to defend that it's not about the money. I just have to do my best and know I'm a good person. If they can't see that, it is not my job to cure their blindness. Personally, I think they say these things because they *know* we're good people and therefore know how to try to hurt us. They think they're in a position of power over us because we politely try to speak reason to their unreasonable demands. They're bullies. Recognize them. Treat them as such. Don't just tell them to go to hell, give them a map and directions. It is not okay to continue to be abused by people.

Clients lie. Not all clients. But many of them. If you're generous, sometimes they're not outright lying, they're telling you their perspective on the truth. When you get a history, it's a nuanced history. Clients lie for many reasons. Some try to minimize the symptoms, in case you try to get them to do something outlandish, like actually diagnose the problem. Some won't tell you things that they actually know – often about dietary indiscretions or drugs the pet could have been given or gotten ahold of. They won't tell you their role in causing a problem; it'll be a complete mystery to them how their dog came up lame, for instance, or if they didn't give prescribed medications properly. You'll never know exactly how long a problem has been going on, just what they'll admit to. The coughing can't be because of smoking in the house, because the owner just told you they only sit by the window and blow the smoke outside. Now, I live in the south, and I know for a fact, no one is doing that in the middle of summer. You'll find that there will be A LOT that you don't know. Especially when you're talking about behavior issues. There are things going on in households that directly affect the psyche, behavior, and health of pets, but you will never know about it; the yelling in a dysfunctional family, the individual mental health issues, etc. It could also be that an owner interprets things differently than us and doesn't think something important to mention. And that's just on the medical side. When I have had to deal with owners outraged at something that happened at our practice, I have had them give entirely different renditions of a situation or conversation. Now, if I were inclined, I could couch it in terms of "misunderstanding" or "miscommunication" or "misperception" and maybe I could have done better at understanding and communicating. Some clients use this unsurety on our parts against us. They also use our natural empathetic propensity against us.   And people can be quite aggressive in promoting their particular "reality". True, I can't often tell if they're being truthful in the belief of their viewpoint or simply skewing the truth knowing full-well, themselves, what they're doing. After all these years, though, I suspect the latter much more often. I've been in many conversations where only through advanced yoga techniques could a person twist the truth into what they're saying happened.

Keep the lying issue and perception issues in mind when owners speak about other veterinarians, which they'll mainly do to malign them, not praise them. If something seems amiss in their presentation of history or treatment regime, that's because there is. They'll say that they followed everything the previous vet said without results. They'll say they've "tried everything". Verbally, they'll give you a remarkably candid and detailed history of the pet's problems, all to no avail. Then you'll get the history from the other vet which shows exactly one visit with no follow-up from several years prior. Same goes for if they tell you what horrid treatment they received at their previous vet; so far, 100% of these, when I got the complete story, was the client being horrid to the previous practice. Don't be too quick to condemn a colleague based on what a client says happened. Don't be too quick to take offense, either, if a client tells you how they took their pet elsewhere and the veterinarian said you did everything wrong. So far, 100% of the time, the client has just been taking a jab, hiding their own words as coming from an authority figure. They think we don't talk to one another. I've had many an amusing conversation with fellow vets about how Mrs. Smith told me you said so-and-so and what do you know? It wasn't so.

One of my favorite situations to witness is the changing of the history. Especially if a couple are involved. I've seen this played out several times. Pet is brought in, owners report vomiting, diarrhea, not eating over several days.   I present bloodwork, radiographs, possible hospitalization. Then, ever so quickly, ever so subtly, a look is exchanged between them. Just a look. No words. And then one will say, "You know what, though? He did eat a little this morning." The other will add, "And I haven't seen him vomit since yesterday morning." The next thing you know, the dog, miraculously, doesn't actually have a problem and they decide they'll just keep an eye on him at home. This sub-textual communication between couples is a wonder to behold.

   Another type of client you'll run into is the "there's finally enough wrong" client. The pet has been intermittently vomiting for months, has weight loss, is lethargic, but now he's limping and is brought in to be seen. You think you're just going to be evaluating a lameness and the next thing you know a whole history of calamities are being trotted out. Just recently had an owner bringing their pet in for an ear infection detected by their groomer. Oh, by the way, that cough from three years ago never got better and it's actually been worse the last several months. Ends up the pet has heart disease and fluid in the lungs. How long? Who knows? This type of behavior is another aspect of passive neglect you'll see all too often.

No, Mrs. Roberts, I don't think holding BooBoo up to the phone so I can listen to her will help. You need to bring her in so I can......(sigh)....Hi, BooBoo...how are you?

2002
Flea allergy.
No, it isn't.
2003
Flea allergy.
Can't be. Doesn't have fleas.
2004
Still flea allergy.
We use flea control!
gnaw gnaw
gnaw gnaw
2005
FLEA ALLERGY.....
He's fine.
scoot scoot
2006
It's flea allergy!
It's not that bad.
2007
sigh flea allergy.
He's not itchy.
2008
Give me an "F"! Give me an "L"!
Never had a flea!
2009
Here's more info. on flea allergy.
We put stuff on it that helps.
2010
FLEA ALLERGY!!
He barely ever scratches.
gnaw gnaw gnaw gnaw gnaw gnaw
We think it's time to put him down.
2011
Well, you won't have to worry about flea allergy anymore!

The three stages of client interactions

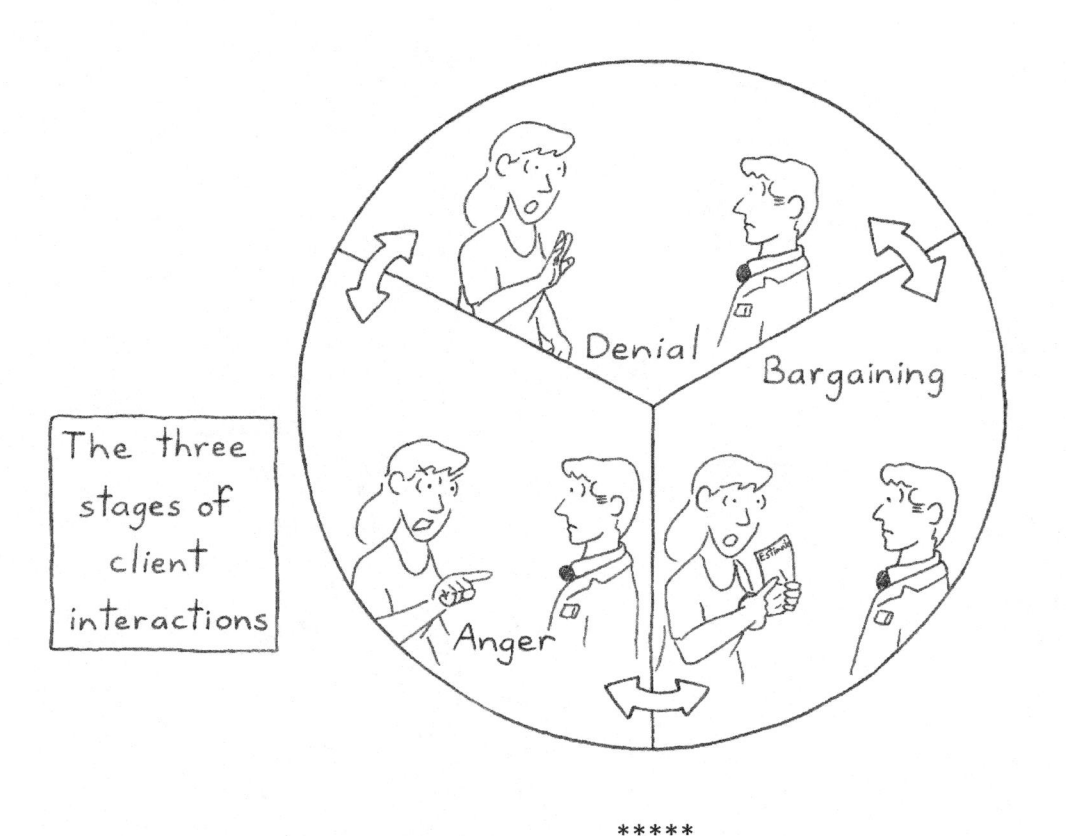

Denial • Bargaining • Anger

Acceptance must be around here somewhere

*****

"I don't know, Doc. I had some fishin' line, a couple of paper clips, and a can of Raid, but it's just not gettin' better!"

The MacGyver Client

My Uncle's cousin's neighbor's friend knew a guy who was the brother of someone who worked at a vet's and *HE* said.....

*****

"The first thing we need to do is some in-house bloodwork and x-rays."

"The first thing we need to do is" *crumple* *crumple*

Pull!

BOOM!

What else can we do?

"I stopped going to my last vet because he kept on insisting on bloodwork every year to refill Spaz's seizure medication!"

"So, you left your last vet because, basically, they had standards."

*****

The Spousal Gambit — where one agrees to things but the other one is who comes later with complaints

He likes tangerines. He's a Virgo.
He was the middle child in his litter.
He's more of a morning-dog.

History we want and history we get are two different things

*****

Hey! You're my dog's vet! That was some accident you were in! Let me ask you a question. My dog, Missy, she's a Pomeranian and she's been coughing a lot lately. What do you think that is?

Is he a bad man?! Is he a bad doctor who's going to hurt you?! Yes he is! He's a bad man! Evil! He's the devil-spawn of Satan who's going to hurt my pookie-wookie!

People who say what they really want to say through their pets

*****

I think it's time to mow.

Should we get the car in for servicing?

I lost <u>another</u> tooth? I guess I should see a dentist eventually.

Should we get him to a vet?

Let's give it another day.

Clients and their other responsibilities

which then became a rash. We, of course, had no idea what Grandpa was doing, otherwise we would have told him to stop. And my cousin's cat had a similar problem, so we used the medication that he had left over from three years before. Because his cat had died, you see. Not because of the problem, but due to an unfortunate piano incident. Well, that seemed to work for a little while and then school started and I got a new job and the car broke down, so we just didn't notice until toys started to disappear. Whenever he's sick, he hides toys. We don't know why. Have you ever heard of such a thing before? We thoug̶ ̶̶̶̶was cute the first time it happened, until we noticed he got down to three pounds, but this was q̶ ̶̶̶̶hile ago. My mom had thought ̶̶̶̶ be due to the weather, since its been so hot lately and ̶̶̶̶ also changed his food, so we ̶̶̶̶e air-conditioning down to 60 and went back to food ̶̶̶̶d from years ̶̶̶̶. But, my mom ̶̶̶̶tis started acting up because it was so cold in the hous̶ ̶̶he had to ̶̶ ̶̶ the ̶ospital for ̶̶̶̶ with pneumonia. Oh, I forgot to tell you! We found ̶ ̶e cat toys i̶ ̶̶̶̶pa's room ̶̶̶̶lized it wasn't Ozzy who had been hiding them, it v̶ ̶̶̶̶̶na! So, f̶ ̶̶̶̶le, we fig̶ ̶̶̶e Ozzy was ok since he wasn't showing his normal s̶ ̶̶̶̶̶̶̶g ̶̶̶̶was more diarrhea than usual. But, his nose was moi̶ ̶̶̶̶̶̶m. Is there anything ̶̶̶̶̶t ̶̶̶̶g? Moist would seem ok unless that means he has a ̶̶̶̶̶uld we have given hi̶̶ c̶̶ ̶̶̶̶we turned the air-conditioning down? And warm co̶ ̶̶̶̶̶̶ a fever, too, couldn't it? W̶ ̶̶̶̶. Maybe it was moist and cold. Oh, I just can't remem̶ ̶̶̶̶aybe you can check his nose ̶ ̶̶̶̶.ell what's wrong. I'm not sure if I'll be able to afford m̶ ̶̶̶̶n just checking his nose. I'm̶ ̶̶̶̶de of money and I don't want this to get into the thousan̶ ̶̶̶̶ollars! After all, with the c̶ ̶̶̶̶king down, our electricity bill went through the roof, my ̶ ̶̶̶̶hospital stay, and Grandpa ̶̶̶̶ to go into a group home now. It's just too much! That ̶ ̶̶̶s me. I have a similar rasl̶ ̶̶̶̶zzy - could you look at it and is it possible for me to just ̶̶̶̶same medication you'll h̶ ̶̶̶̶r him? Because my new job doesn't offer any insurance an̶ ̶̶̶̶̶s' daddy hasn't paid m̶ ̶̶̶̶l support or alimony in six months! Do you think he could ha̶ ̶̶̶ght the rash from me? H̶ ̶̶̶ps in my bed every night. I'm talking about Ozzy, not my kids' daddy. Which leads me

*****

Client Logic

"So, I have a stupid question."

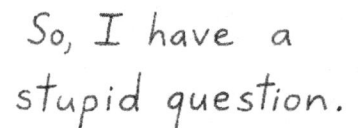

"Lucky for you I specialize in stupid questions. I've had a lot of practice."

*****

"He just needs his rabies. He doesn't need an exam. He's healthy. No problems."

"Hey, Doc, since you're here. Could you take a quick non-chargeable look at this lump I **just** found?"

Client Tactics: The Fake-Out

He's indoors only.	He's not around other cats.
He's been vaccinated for it.	I know he's healthy.
I don't want to know if it's positive.	It doesn't matter anyway since there's no treatment
So...... that's a 'No' for doing the FeIV/FIV test?	And it's too expensive.

Some clients believe in a good defense

*****

Take this — there's an angry client in the lobby.

"What do you mean you're going to charge me for a urinalysis? I only brought the urine in because the doctor asked me to. I was doing him a favor!"

"Why are you charging me again when the first treatment didn't work?!"

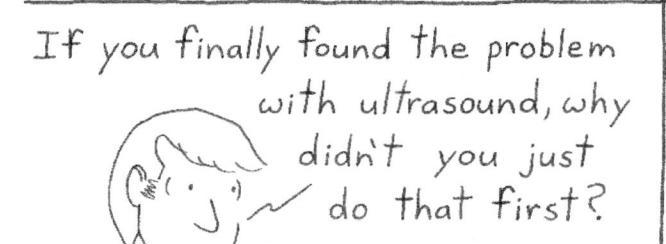

"If you finally found the problem with ultrasound, why didn't you just do that first?"

"Those medications you gave on my dog's exam last year never worked!"

Client Logic Continued

*****

"I really admire your optimism! You keep thinking I'm going to do something."

"So, here's '08 and '09. Then it goes to '03. Well, that's too far back. Wait! Here's the most recent! No, that's 2011. That's strange. Here's another '08......"

you should see the house

Why can't clients put medical records in order on their own time?

*****

"What's the schedule like today?"

"Let's see, our first one is ADR, then we have "acting strange", a "weird behavior", and "not normal." Then, NAR, "seems different," "acting odd", a "new idiosyncracy," and a WTF."

"Sooooo..... the usual."

"Well, it can't be allergies, because she's never had allergies before."

"He got his shots two weeks ago and now he's vomiting."

"Ma'am, you can't have pills left over if I gave you 30, three months ago, and you've given one a day since."

"Well, I have given one EVERYDAY! And she's still not better!"

"I want to get to the bottom of this problem as long as it doesn't cost more than $50."

More Client Logic
*****

"I know nothing! Nothing!"

Some clients like to pull a "Sergeant Schultz"*

*for those of you under 40, Google "Hogan's Heroes Sergeant Schultz"

| January | April | August |

| December | February | No, it's too big to remove. We don't want to put him through that. |

*****

"We'd like to use a menu from a different restaurant. And can you change the music in here? Also, we're going to be here way past your closing time. Could you not wait on other tables while we're here? We're going to be paying in Euros also, so if you could check the exchange rate for us that would be great. Why haven't we received our food yet?"

Clients out at dinner

"I will gladly pay you Tuesday for a diagnosis today."

The 'Wimpy' Client

*****

"Any problems?"

"He's been coughing."

"OK. We'll probably need to find......"

"Oh, it's a problem, but I don't necessarily want to do anything about it."

2013: He's really due for a dental cleaning. — No.

2014: ...and he has a lot of tartar on his teeth. — No.

2015: Still needs a dental. — No.

2016: ...and it's just like when we get our teeth done! — No.

2017: Dental month is next month! You'll get a discount! — No.

2018: Clean teeth means good health. — He's too old to get his teeth done now.

*****

I'm sorry. Yes, I'm a vet. But I don't hold a specialty in pet peeves.

Client Encounter of the First Kind:

visual sighting from less than 500 feet away;
evasion and escape still possible;
know your exits

Client Encounter of the Second Kind:

recognition acknowledged by eye contact,
wave, salutation, gun-play, etc.;
evasion and escape less likely unless
reliance placed on instinctual survival responses
or serious pre-training has occurred

Client Encounter of the Third Kind:

contact; all hope lost; resistance futile;
possible consequences may include but
not limited to communication,
social abduction, and probing

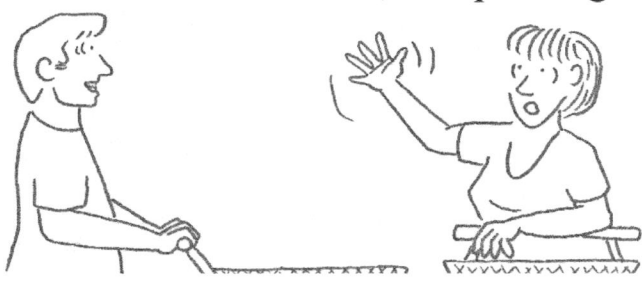

Panel 1: "and once we get blood results we'll need to....." — "He eats dirt!"

Panel 2: "Let me go through this estimate and explain...." — "His nose is warm!"

Panel 3: "What we do in this procedure is...." — "She likes broccoli!"

Panel 4: "while he's in the hospital we'll...." — "Why does he shed so much?"

How are we supposed to give information to some owners so they can make "informed" decisions?

*****

"Please let me treat your pet! Pleeeaassse! I can make him better! Just let me do something!"

Anyone else ever feel this way?

Client Logic: Why not to do things

Heartworm Prevention
We don't need it because we have birds in our yard that eat the mosquitos.

Microchipping
If he can't find his way home, then there's something wrong with him.

Bordetella Vaccine
If he ever gets sick from it, I will too.

Parvo Vaccine
Her puppies don't need it because she got sick with it when she was a puppy, so her immunity will protect them.

*****

— All this prescription says is "Common Sense".

— Yes. And I think you should get that filled immediately.

Before the exam

"Any problems at all?"

"Nope. Everything's good!"

After the exam

"Okay! He checks out just fine!"

"Aha! You didn't say anything about this ¼" skin tag under his armpit!"

Client Tactics: The Pop Quiz

*****

"...Kidney disease...blahblahblah... elevated BUN and creatine...Kidney enzymes...blah blah...special Kidney-sparing diet...blahblah...recheck kidney values..."

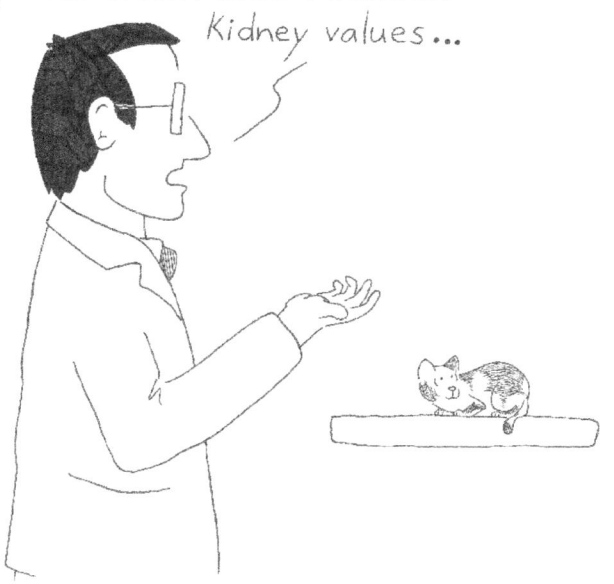

"So, this is a liver problem?"

He vomits 2-3 times everyday, has diarrhea, and hasn't eaten in a week.

We should start with x-rays and bloodwork. He may need to be hospitalized.

Now that I think about, he hasn't vomited in the past two weeks. And he did eat this morning and had a normal poop, so he's probably fine.

Client Tactics: The History Reversal

*****

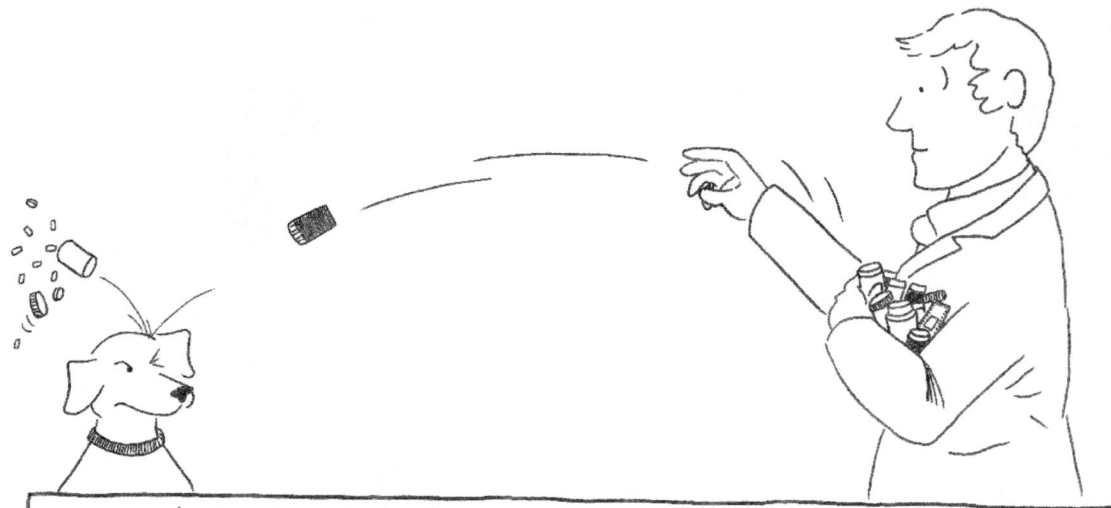

What I think of when clients tell me previous vets didn't fix the problem, they just "threw antibiotics at him".

Clients in other situations

"My baby's been throwing up for three days. What can I do at home to get him to stop?" — Pediatrician

"My car's been making a 'bwrrr bwrrr' sound at around 30 miles an hour? What do you think that is?" — Car Mechanic

"I've read every self-help book and blog and haven't been able to help myself. I know you're not telling me what I can just do at home because you want my money from an appointment!" — Psychiatrist

"My house is on fire and I've been spitting on it for 20 minutes and it's not working. What should I do?" — Fire Department

*****

"Bloodwork. Bloodwork. Bloodwork."

"So, you don't recommend doing anything?"

"But it's never happened before!"

Client Logic: Reason given when client doesn't believe what you've said.

*****

"I will continue to say 'Ni' to you until you appease us!"

Ni! Ni! Ni!

The Clients Who Say "Ni!"

He's on heartworm every month. He's up to date on all his shots. We don't give him people food. He's on flea control. He's a good dog and doesn't bite. This problem he has now has only been going on for two days.

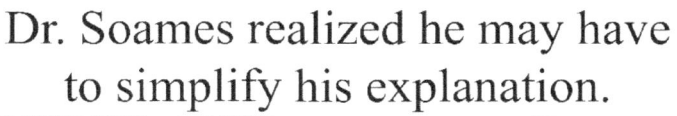

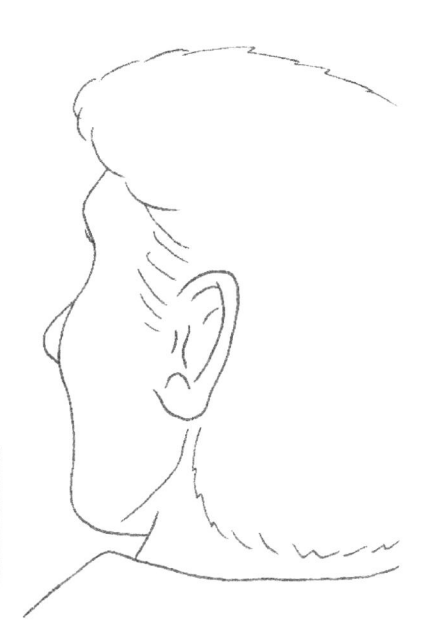

The Pinocchio Client

*****

Dr. Soames realized he may have to simplify his explanation.

It's a simple question, Mr. Anderson! How long has this problem been going on?!
You'll never get me to talk! Never!
Ever feel like you're interrogating a client?

*****

blah blah blah... holistic.... blah blah... alternative medicine... blahblahblah .... seven herbs and spices... blah blah blah.... all-natural... blah blah
We have Harry Potter wands we sell up front that work as well as that stuff.

We should FelV/FIV test him.	But he's an indoor cat.	Have you had him tested before?	Um. Yeah. And it was negative.	When was that?	Oh. Ah. When he was a kitten.
Give me the clinic's name where it was done and we can update your file.	I don't remember the name.	I see. Was it local? If you can tell us where it was I'm sure we can figure it out.		Look. I'm lying, oK? You know it. I certainly know it. Let's just move on!	

*****

He's had that his whole life. He's too old to fix it now.

bilateral entropion

Well, yes. If you wait long enough on anything, they eventually become too old to fix.

DVM
University of Idahno

Why does it seem the least qualified person is the one to bring the pet in?

*****

That's not the problem.

Ooookay. Well, what do you think the problem is?

I don't know! That's why I brought him to you!

Yes, and I told you what.....

That's not the problem.

yak yak yak yak yak yak yak
blah blah blah blah blah blah blah blah blah blah blah blah blah blah blah
I want a toy and I want it NOW!
blah blah blah blah blah blah blah blah blah
Who's my pumpkin? You are! Yes you are! My little pumpkin!
blah blah blah blah blah blah blah blah blah blah blah blah
You don't know what you're talking about!
It's been three months not two!
I did not do that!
If you'd empty the litterbox more often!
blah blah blah blah blah
... and that's why treatment is important.
Things people do in rooms other than listen to you

*****

crab crab crab
First Visit
complain complain complain
Second Visit
argue argue argue
Third Visit
crab argue complain
Fourth Visit
What will it take from me to get you to go elsewhere? Because I'm willing to do it!
Fifth Visit

Is he current on his vaccines?

I don't know.

How long has he been sick?

I don't know.

Any vomiting or diarrhea?

I don't know.

Well, what do you know?

The Jon Snow Client

*****

Hey..... I'm really sorry to bother you but I know you're a vet and one of my reindeer can't fly. Can you come take a quick look at him?

Client Expectations

We are constantly told to meet or exceed client expectations. But do we really think about what that means? We do recalls, offer coffee in the lobby, have email for client questions, give out our cell phone number, have extended hours. We're like a gushing water main of endless pleasing. These are more like ideas that are kind of neat; they may or may not address expectations. What do you expect when you go somewhere? When I go to a restaurant, I expect to eat reasonably priced food in a timely manner with a pleasant ambience. Do I need all of these to be met or exceeded? No. Admittedly, I'm pretty easy to please. I actually assume things will go wrong, so when things go well, my expectations were exceeded! Yay!

The point here is you don't know what your clients expect. Clients do not come in and tell you what they expect. There's absolutely no way to know what they are thinking. You only hear about expectations retroactively. Any changes we make in our behavior or protocols to address missing a particular client's expectation are therefore all retroactive. Which may not even apply to future interactions with that same client, much less other clients; expectations are situational and ever-changing. I think we're too reactive when it comes to trying to meet everyone's demands of the moment. There is always going to be someone who is inconvenienced by situations you have little control over, as well as those whose outlandish expectations will never be met no matter how hard you try.

I don't know what to make of exceeding expectations as an expression. Besides not knowing what a client's expectations are in the first place, it begs the question, how far do you have to exceed expectations? I harken back to the one vet school that requires 500 hours of volunteer/animal experience but suggests to exceed expectations one should do 2,000. Or more. Where does the pursuit of exceeding expectations end?

We can presume things. We are geared to continue adding to this ever-growing list of things for clients that may or may not actually address an individual's expectations. Let's use one example. Offering coffee in the lobby. I don't drink coffee, so this does nothing for me. Sure, a broad part of the population may be served with this offering. Shouldn't we offer alternatives, however? What about tea? Soda, bottled water, diet drinks, fruit drinks? After all, meeting or exceeding expectations means you're trying to meet or exceed everyone's expectations, not just a certain segment of the populace, but every individual. I'm sure you can see, with just this one example, and a non-medical, service one at that, it is impossible and we are setting ourselves up for failure with a false premise and unreasonable goal. I still remember the client who grumbled that we didn't have their preferred creamer for the coffee. Not a Starbucks, dude!

In one advice column I read that if you aren't doing X, Y, and Z, the client will just go down the street to a different practice. Some clients don't like the door closed when they're in the exam room. Some don't want to be separated from their pet at any point. Some want to be ushered straight into a room and not be in the waiting area. Some people like for you to talk with them a lot. Some people want to keep it short and simple. The list of wants, needs, and whims we deal with in a particular day with the general public is already daunting. Now we want to preemptively figure out what those wants, needs, and whims might be? Good luck. When you address things that clients do tell you, then you are accommodating them, which is just a nice and polite thing to do, as long as you aren't inconveniencing others and it's something reasonable. Sometimes they're not. Sometimes you will not be able to accommodate for whatever reason. People need to learn to be able to deal with disappointment. Client wants to be in surgery with their dog? Nope. Not in my practice. I am not going to come near meeting that expectation. Too bad. Feel free to see if you can find another practice if you need that itch scratched. Client wants my cell phone number because their previous vet gave them theirs? Not going to happen. Feel free to return to that previous vet. And that's if I even believe what they're telling me is true, not just a ploy to get me to comply.

This ever-present feeling that we are going to upset a client by not giving them everything they want needs to stop. We go through these paroxysms trying to please clients and all we're really doing is raising expectations. If we're continuing to raise expectations, will we ever meet, much less exceed them? If you call an owner back within minutes, they now have an expectation that is always going to happen. There will come a time where you may not be able to get back with them until the end of the day or tomorrow. Now you have a ticked-off owner. It can make you crazy trying to figure out the "right" approach. I'm not saying just throw up your hands and give up trying to please people. There are always ways to improve, just be selective in what you do. Set standards and protocols that you are comfortable with and find fair to you, your staff, and your clients. Some people will be pleased, some won't. The unfortunate reality is no matter what you do, what you offer, or how you approach people, there's going to be a certain set of people who aren't going to be pleased. The "public" is a voracious, needy, and arbitrary animal that is never sated. Don't make yourself crazy worrying about whether you're doing enough. One of the things I look at is, what do other medical professions do? I don't advocate being like them, but be aware of how much we already do to accommodate clients, far and above our fellow medical professions. The level of service we provide just as a matter-of-course is amazing. And people still voice dissatisfaction. When I go to my doctor, I expect for them to make me feel better. If they meet that expectation, I'm pretty happy. If they make me younger and more fit, then I guess that'd be one way to *exceed* my expectations. Wouldn't it be nice if we got credit for meeting the main expectation of our job – making animals well?

"I thought I was seeing the tall, pretty doctor."

"Yes, well, I thought I was seeing the smart, considerate client. So, I guess we're both disappointed."

*****

"Before I agree to bloodwork, I want to know what you're looking for, what the treatment options are for each potential problem, and estimates for each one as well."

He's not better.

The last time you were here and we discussed treatment, all you said was you'd "consider" it.

What else do you suggest I do?

Well, let's see. You could cogitate, ponder, deliberate. Muse perhaps? One study shows promise with those that proactively contemplate.

*****

So, what you want to do is, wait for them to calm down, then give them attention. You don't want to reward bad behavior.

%#@!☆#⚡!!

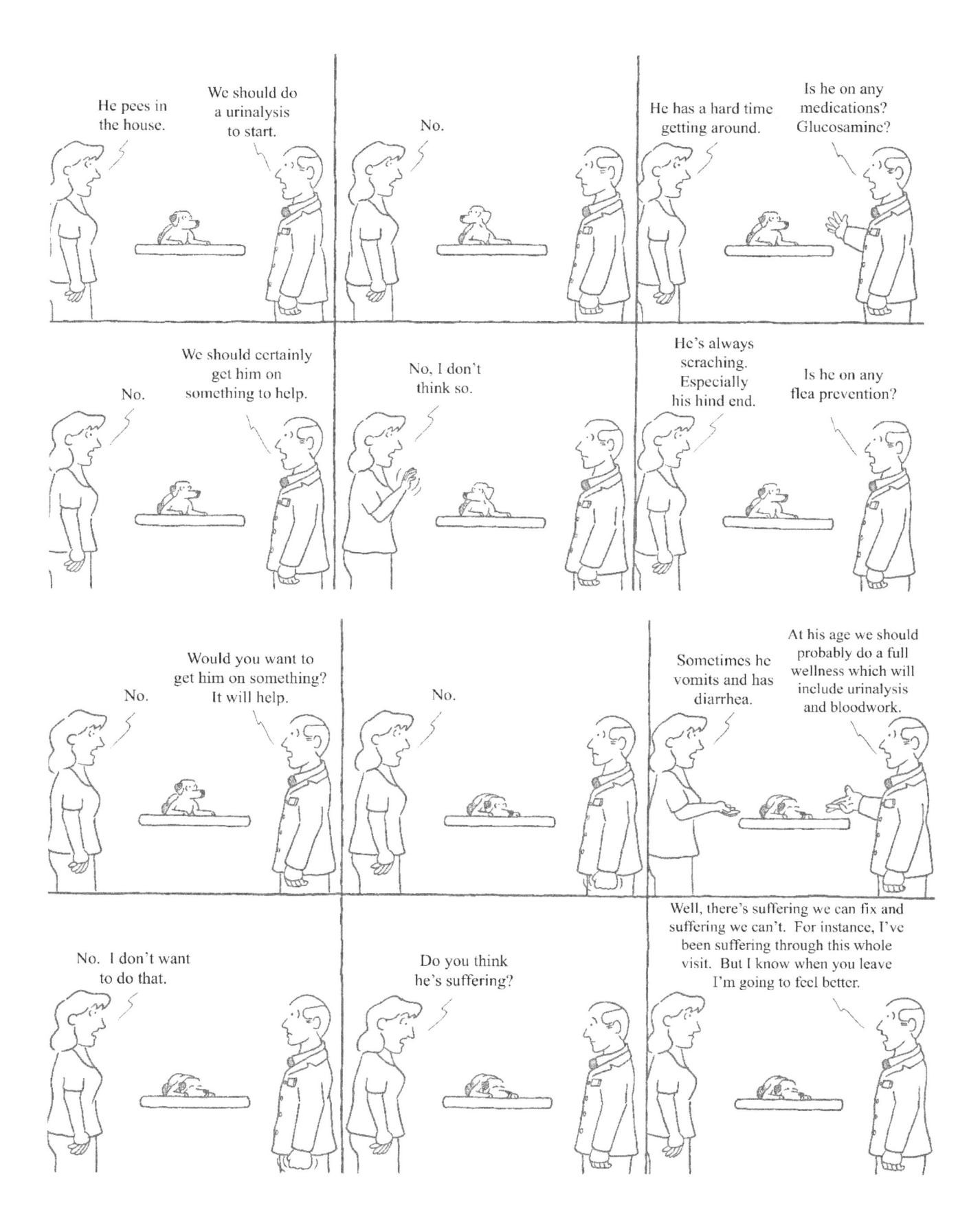

He pees in the house. / **We should do a urinalysis to start.**	**No.**	**He has a hard time getting around.** / **Is he on any medications? Glucosamine?**	
No. / **We should certainly get him on something to help.**	**No, I don't think so.**	**He's always scraching. Especially his hind end.** / **Is he on any flea prevention?**	
No. / **Would you want to get him on something? It will help.**	**No.**	**Sometimes he vomits and has diarrhea.** / **At his age we should probably do a full wellness which will include urinalysis and bloodwork.**	
No. I don't want to do that.	**Do you think he's suffering?**	**Well, there's suffering we can fix and suffering we can't. For instance, I've been suffering through this whole visit. But I know when you leave I'm going to feel better.**	

"I need to get my dog's prescription."
Yes. I see we will have to order it for you.
2 hours later
ring
"Is my prescription ready yet?"
No, sir. As I said before we have to order it.
1½ hours later
ring
"Is my dog's prescription ready now?"
It will be later this week, sir. We will call you when it comes in.
1 hour later
ring
"How about now?"
Still no.
½ hour later
ring
"Is it going to be in today?"
No.
15 minutes later...
ring
NO!

"Don't you work at the vet clinic? I'm so glad I ran into you. Would you mind trimming Bitsy's nails? It won't take but a minute."

BAKERY NEEDS
SPICES
PICKLES
CONDIMENTS
PICNIC ITEMS
3

*****

"OK! Start your diagnosis...... NOW!"

Step 1: The Dr. Explains	Step 2: Technician Explains	Step 3: Informative Handouts
Step 4: Tests and options reviewed again	Step 5: Recalls and Follow-ups	Mrs. Smith still has questions. Step 6: Return to Step 1

*****

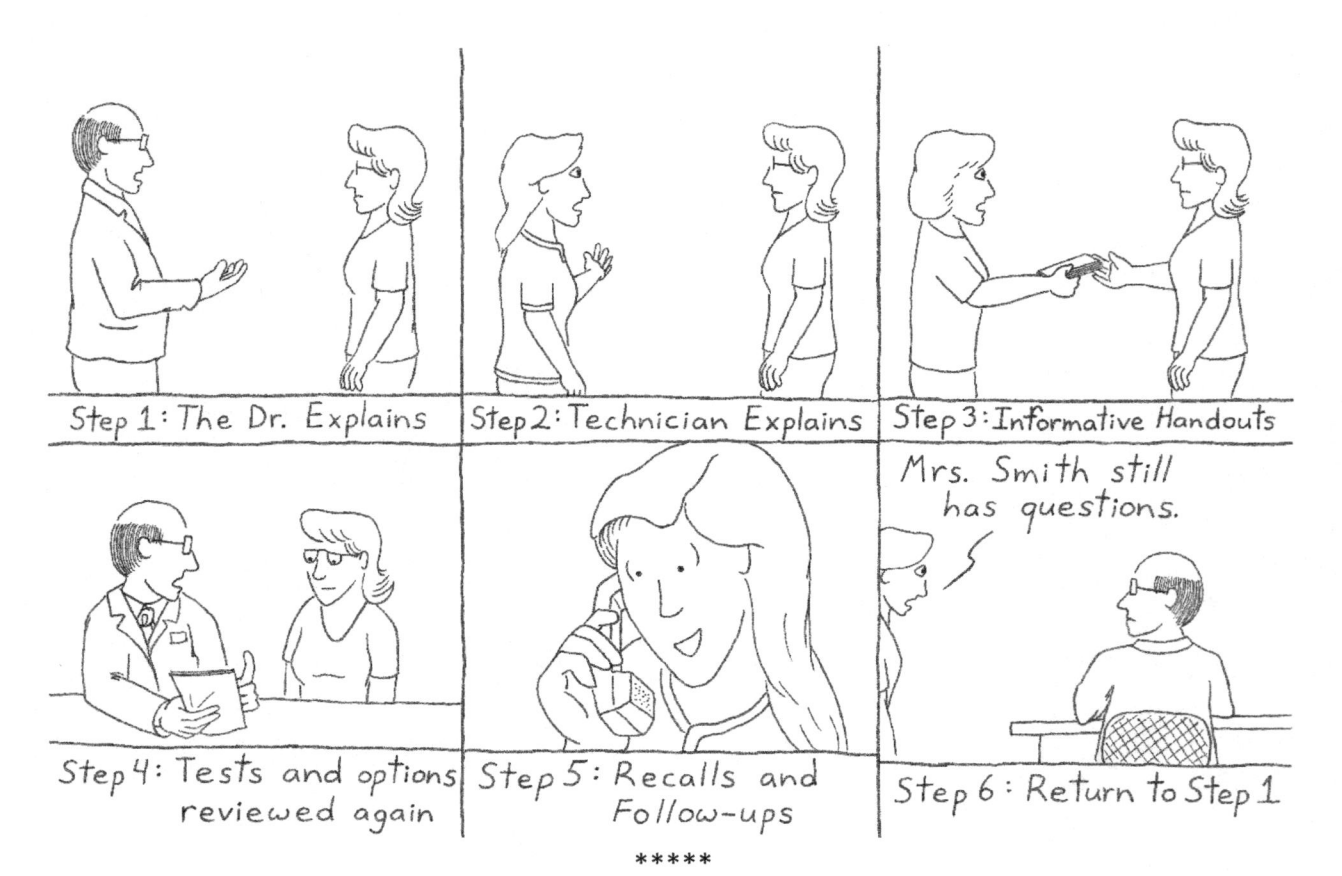

"My other dog was vomiting and having diarrhea two weeks ago. Why do you think that happened?"

"Well, I could answer that but I might cause a rift in the space/time continuum. And I just can't risk that."

Why have I been made to wait so long?!

Of the three appointments before you, one was late, another scheduled puppy boosters but brought in a different and very sick older pet instead, and the third wanted to have one pet seen but talk about behavior problems in two pets who weren't here. Here are the names and phone numbers of those clients. Please feel free to take your complaints up with them.

* * * * *

I want you to find the easiest thing for us to treat.

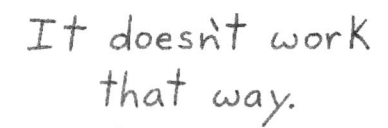

It doesn't work that way.

He continues to have anxiety and old dog mental issues.

Your previous vet put him on some medications. They're not working?

No, they work. I just don't give them.

?

I just want him to be better without medication.

*****

With all your education, why weren't you able to see the future?!

Because I went to a school where Ouija boards, palm reading, and Tarot cards weren't part of the curriculum.

"$300?! That's outrageous! I must be in the wrong business!"

"If you actually proceeded with this estimate, you would have spent a total of $370 here in the eight years you've had this cat. I'm pretty sure you couldn't live on $46 a year."

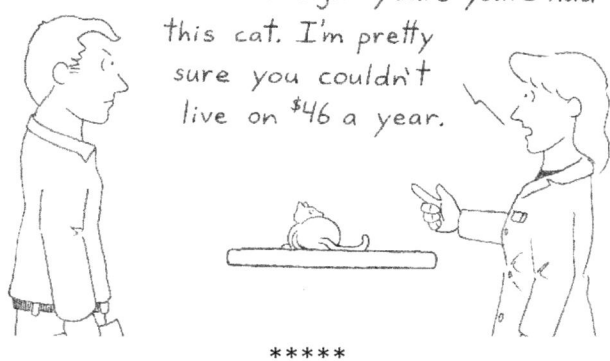

*****

"You said he'd die of the cancer before the heartworm disease, but you were wrong!"

Panel 1
"Is he still vomiting?" "No."

Panel 2
"Diarrhea?" "No."

Panel 3
"Then, how is he not better?"

Panel 4
"He's still 14!"

*****

Panel 5
[Wednesday]
"We should have results by tomorrow."

Panel 6
Thursday, 12:01 AM
"...please leave a message. ¡beeeeep¡"
"I was told my dog's tests would be back today and I haven't heard from anyone! Don't you people even care how worried I am! I expect a call, from the doctor, immediately!"

Step 1:
We will need to do surgery to check out those lumps.

Step 2:
That worries me. I don't want to do any anesthesia.

Step 3:
Then don't do the surgery.

Step 4:
But, I want to know what the lumps are.

...return to Step 1 and repeat

*****

I have issues to bring up that happened at my last visit here!

Your one and only visit here was five years ago.

Yes! And that's what I have questions about!

He's only had this tumor for two years! Fix it! Now!

*****

These meds you gave my dog didn't work!
How often did you use them?
Once a week!
These are labeled for twice a day.
It doesn't matter what they're labeled – they don't work!

Give insulin any time as long as it's at least twice a day. I can feed any kind of food as long as I feed him the diabetic diet also. It's ok to skip a dose to save money and make the bottle last longer. There's no need for a recheck as long as he seems fine. If I see anything strange with him I can adjust the dose based on planetary positioning.

OK, I understand that's what you heard, but that's not what I said.

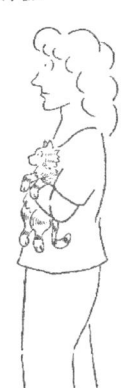

*****

Yes, this problem can be complicated. If it were simple, I wouldn't be called doctor.

"I don't understand why you won't refill his eye meds! They didn't work anyway!"

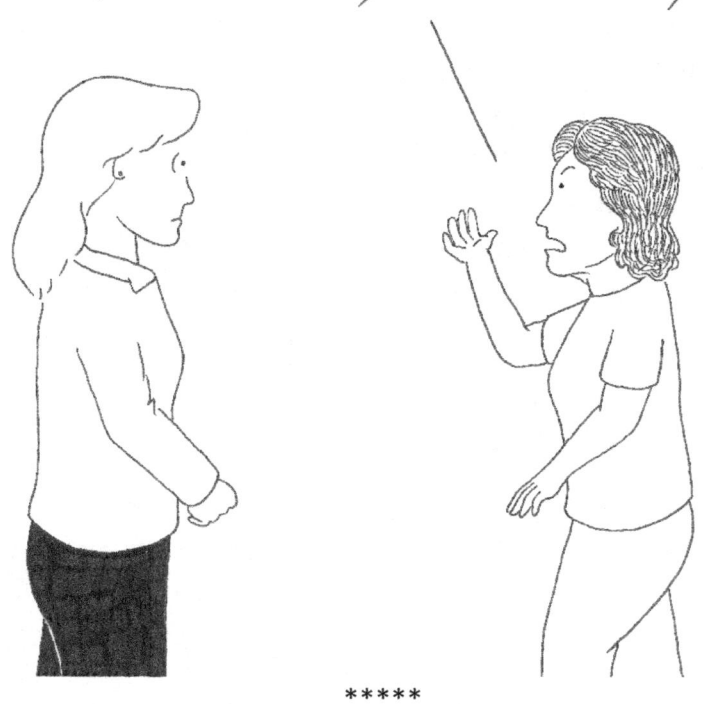

*****

"Heartworm pills? I don't want to do anything that will prolong his life."

Here's the pharmacy, Mrs. Jones. Why don't you just pick out whatever you think you need.

Client Loyalty

Client loyalty is a myth. And it's one we buy into because so many people talk about having it and keeping it and nurturing it. Client loyalty is short-hand for doing anything and everything to retain a client. It is very one-sided. The myth is that if we attend diligently and properly to every need a client may have, they will stay with us forever. This isn't true and its propagation can have a corrosive influence on us. If we are open 24 hours a day for the convenience of our clients, schedule things according to their ever-changing needs and balance the expectations of every one of them so as not to create overlap or conflict, and put all of them first forever, we will arrive at the magical destination called "Client Loyalty". And it is a mirage. And we will have killed ourselves walking across a desert obstacle course striving for it. True loyalty is freely given. "Client Loyalty" is negotiable and you can be held hostage by clients in exchange for loyalty. You still provide good service, put your best advice out there, help people and animals in need; that's the whole point of our job. Just don't do those things or feel you need to do more to retain the ephemera called "client loyalty". You will have a percentage of clients that will go nowhere else, it's true. They want to see you and have your expertise. This has little to do with you and more to do with them. There will always be a percentage of clients that like you, don't like you, feel neutral, regardless of what you do or don't do. Our profession has mentally suffered from the advice of so-called consultants who prey on our wanting to be liked and be successful, pointing at ways to achieve that and also pointing out what they consider our "faults". We're constantly told we need to do more and that's an indefinite journey on a path of diminishing returns.

We buy-in to this fantasy of mollifying every client's little eccentricity. Clients like nothing better than to tell us what they like or don't like. In my first five years out I personally did recalls, I gave follow-up material and explained things to five different relatives, arranged special times to help some people out, amongst many other things. All appreciated by the clients at the time, I'm sure. It was also an endless endeavor. Meanwhile, the litany of things clients expressed dissatisfaction about mounted as well.

We've heard that a client will only travel about 3 – 5 miles to a veterinarian. This is in direct opposition to the definition of "client loyalty". It means convenience comes first. It means you're being chosen mainly by whether they drive by your practice or not. It also means that should your client move even a little bit away, they'll be going to see someone else. Here's the thing. That's ok. Other clients will move in to the area. It is not a reflection on you. And it doesn't require you to start doing more than you already are. Yes, we can always improve. However, "client loyalty", as a coin of the realm, is fool's gold. I've found when a client decides to go elsewhere, it is mainly based on caprice and whim. I've had people who I've seen for decades just decide to go somewhere else for a "change". Perhaps that's just what they told us, but it seemed honest, if a bit dismissive, as if they were trying a new Thai restaurant rather than choosing medical care. I told a long-standing client "no" to something once. Now they don't see me. I had another long-term client with multiple pets who I had consistently gone out of my way for, leave. These are situations that will have nothing to do with you and everything to do with your clients' psychology. We generate no credit with people. You can have done nine-hundred things for them, but don't do one thing or do one thing they don't like and that is what they'll judge you on. You can't control people. *They* don't even know what they need or want.

There seems to be an unsettling outlook that all clients are created equal, that all complaints are legitimate and valid, and that we must "fix" something whenever these things come up. That sounds to my ears like we're in an abusive relationship with clients. In my career, I would say that less than 2 percent of client complaints are legitimate. That doesn't mean to say I'm perfect 98 percent of the time—it means we deal with a whole lot of complaints. That's because that's what people do. Just because a client is angry doesn't mean they're right. I see a lot of management and owners running scared because a client complains. They also unfairly lay the blame on associates and staff. That's what the client wants. It's learned behavior. Don't reward it. You just create monsters that way. And I am completely aware of this as a repeating theme.

I've been in the unenviable situation of having an emergency when a long-time client also came in, unannounced, and demanded to see only me. Even with an explanation given and being seen by another doctor and attended to, they didn't get what they wanted. They had us send their records to another practice. Think about this for a moment. They only wanted to see me. This is the very essence of client loyalty. And once, due to unusual circumstances, they were unable to, their answer was to go somewhere else, ensuring that they'll never see me again. This seems illogical unless you understand it wasn't the neglect to their frail, fragile loyalty that caused this decision, but rather that they didn't get their way once. In other words, this "loyalty" we speak of so much is a phantasm, fleeting and fickle. Not really loyalty at all.

The insidious dilemma about "client loyalty" is, if you believe in it, the situations I presented above can seem like personal failures. They're not. There will be times you have to insist on a follow-up appointment or to re-run bloodwork on a long-term case, or present an invoice for a procedure the client can get done cheaper elsewhere. You will have to tell clients "no". And they can be a bit like children; they don't like the word "no". If you say "yes" to everything, pursuing "client loyalty", you may have fewer adverse encounters, but you will also over-extend, financially, emotionally, and professionally. You will do yourself and your principles a disservice. Set the standards that you can live with, not those others set for you. Don't be pressured into things you don't wish to do because of clients' wishes.

Client Perceptions

We are told that we are supposed to behave and operate in a certain way so we are not misperceived by clients. Good luck with that. Regardless of anything else you've heard, you cannot control client perceptions. You can speak clearly. You can explain things fully. You can modulate your tone in an agreeable way, use "mirroring" techniques and body language to convey compassion, empathy, and understanding. And still, if a client is inclined, you and your staff can be misperceived or purposefully misinterpreted.

People misperceive all the time. Often, they're not paying attention or they're putting what's going on around them through their own personal filter. How often do we hear, "No one ever told me that."? Well, yes, we actually told you three different times. I'm never sure if clients are expressing their perception of a situation or they know full well what the truth is but they aren't going to admit to it and are just committing to the blame game. Owners often don't even see us do things in rooms. "Oh, you already gave the shot?" is heard very commonly. Even though we did it right in front of them or even stated what we were doing. I had one owner who took us to task for not doing something in a room which we had done and then went on to accuse us of having done something we didn't do. How do you reason with someone whose reality is different than yours? Answer: you don't. You can explain things, but ultimately people will believe what they think they saw or heard (or didn't see or hear).

From the columns I've read over the years, when these things happen, we seem to think it's our fault in some manner and we just need to improve our communication skills. Again, though, clients have preconceived notions, they have different histories and experiences that inform their perceptions, and you have no knowledge of what those are and no control over them anyway. Don't get me wrong, you can be perceived positively also. I just don't spend as much time talking about those because they take care of themselves. I've had a client just praise the heck out of me for being the best doctor they've ever had when I gave their dog a rabies vaccination. Yes, yes, I give good rabies. Thanks.

There's also talk about influencing perception. This kind of talk smacks of deception to me. Yes, you can wear something slovenly and people will think such and such about you. You can wear the white jacket and give the impression of authority and professionalism. I'm not a white coat and dress-up kind of person. I find I'm a lot more of a stiff than normal when in such an outfit. What you should do and be is what is comfortable for you and your staff. Otherwise it will just come off as false. To some degree what I'm telling you is to ignore other people's advice as to how you are or are not supposed to be. The only person that can be you with any accuracy is you. Another avenue of influencing perception that I've seen advised is to have personal notes about clients and their family members so you can ask them about family vacations and birthdays and such. Again, not my comfort level. It infers a more intimate relationship than there actually is. I can be friendly with clients, but it's a business relationship, not a friend relationship.

The main reason I'm going on about this at all is that I think we need to give ourselves a break. More often than not I have found client misperception to be more about them than about me, or us. You can't be all things to all people and neither should you try. What you should be is yourself. I am going to be as nice as possible and do the best job I can for a pet and client. I'm going to try to give the same to everyone I see. This may be sufficient for some clients and be found insufficient by others. Too bad. I can only do my best. While I'll try to make allowances for people's behaviors and be accommodating, I'm not going to weary myself by wondering how I'm being perceived or apologizing because someone thought I meant something other than I did. And it's one thing for me, a scarred and ragged veteran of many a conflict, to raise shields to full intensity when dealing with a client's misperceptions. It's another, and this is where my concern deeply lies, when you're new to the profession and experience this. I'll see many new graduates expressing concern that they must not be doing something right because of the way clients are responding negatively to them. Trust me, it's not you, it's them. The entity known as "The Public" is impossible to please. Doesn't mean we shouldn't try, however don't beat yourself up if a client goes off on you and it seems a little bewildering as to why.

I think most of us in the veterinary profession are nice people. We're caregivers and we seek to improve ourselves and provide better service to clients and patients on a regular basis. I think we strive to not offend and if a client encounter turns unsavory, we wonder what we did wrong in that situation. A number of articles I read about negative client encounters seem to encourage an introspective view as to how we could have done better. Never do I really see anyone put blame or responsibility on the client. I'm not sure if it's because we don't want to bite the hand that feeds us. I think that we are often too nice. Since I don't have that problem, here are some things that need to be said.

Clients can be mean. I've had the most hurtful things slung my way. Or toward my staff. Completely unwarranted things. I can feel you, the reader, nodding along with this. We have to be like Superman and let these verbal bullets bounce off of us. I think it's a tactic by clients to make us feel bad. It's like being on the playground in third grade. A client will say "you're in it for the money" or "you don't care about animals" or "you suck" (as one article I read stated). Come on! This isn't adult behavior and we don't need to tolerate it. Or internalize it. Some clients seem to like to get themselves worked-up. I think it might be their primary way of going through life. It's cathartic to them in a way, regardless how it harms or hurts others. Internet reviews are the new way of bullying. Nothing has to be proved to write an internet review. They just have to "feel" wronged. Not actually be wronged.

Clients use bait-and-switch techniques more than what we are accused of doing. One spouse comes in and agrees to things, the other spouse arrives later when everything has been done to rail and complain and insinuate that the other spouse was coerced or fooled in some way by us. I've been thrown under the bus by many spouses who know full-well what was actually discussed. We deal with a lot of proxy owners too. The mother who's pet-sitting for their daughter. The adult son who has been sent to approve treatment and pay. Then the other people in the family arrive all jazzed up and angry to dispute charges and treatment and what should or should not have been done. My opinion? Maybe you should have been present then. And while I don't think these folks are sitting around their living room planning these encounters, I do think that they have been rewarded in a certain way for such behaviors. Heck, maybe they do it deliberately. Either way I see it as a tactic and you shouldn't get bamboozled by such.

Clients will take even the smallest thing and blow it up beyond all reasonable proportions. I have seen people take a small error and work it and massage it until it becomes the worst thing they have ever had done to them. This, too, is a tactic. I watched a guy come in livid from the drive-thru at a Burger King and proceed to bash everyone in sight. And I'm thinking to myself, ok, how much could have gone wrong with his order that he's demanding to see the actual owner of the franchise (who wasn't there at the time) and that the manager who was there and able to deal with his complaint he deemed "useless". Here was someone that I could see in a veterinary setting who uses being angry as justification for anything they say from that point onward. "See? I'm angry! Therefore, I must have been wronged so I can say and act any way I want!" is the way I see their thinking going. This is behavior that has been rewarded throughout their life by people jumping through hoops to make them happy (an impossible task because it's based on a false premise that they can be made happy) simply because they have expressed displeasure. There have been a couple of time I or my staff have seen our own clients out in public, acting in the same untoward way we've been exposed to. Just proves to me that what a lot of these people are doing is an act, possibly ingrained behavior, but still not something appropriate or valid to which we have to cater.

We seem to want to assume complete responsibility for how every client encounter plays out and I don't think that's fair to ourselves. Set your own personal standards of what you deem acceptable behaviors. Evaluate each circumstance for where you or your staff could have done better. But don't assume that just because someone is complaining, that it is legitimate. I have found, more often than not, that while the owner may believe their complaint is valid or want to convince you of its validity, it's usually not. You don't have to accede to a client's version of reality if it is not true. Do we give in because they wear us down? Do we give in because we think it will mollify the situation? Do we give in because we want to be liked? Do we give in because we're afraid that they might say bad things about us? I'm not sure; maybe all of the above. I don't bend to emotional blackmail, whether it's stated or implied. That's an abusive relationship we're building with the client, with us as the victim. I think the more earnest and honest you are, the more likely you are to bend to these abusive techniques from people. Don't. Once people have reached anger mode, they're going to continue to be angry. Mollifying or giving concessions only rewards their behavior. It will not prevent them from saying bad things about you either.

Does the above make you uncomfortable? Does accusing clients of the above seem unfair? Well, maybe I've been hanging out with the wrong clientele. However, I bet you recognize some of the above from your own client encounters. It's just we don't really discuss it amongst ourselves. As if it is some kind of taboo. We may laugh at certain things and share certain situations with each other, but we don't really discuss the abnormal pathologies we have to deal with on a regular basis.

"I come to you because I know you'll always be honest with me!"	"I know you're just telling me stuff to get money out of me! You vets! It's all just a racket!"

Same Doctor – Different Clients

*****

What is really happening	What the client sees
	"What are you doing! You're scaring him!"

We need to run a bile acids test.
Are you sure?
We found crystals in your cat's urine.
Are you sure?
The femur is definitely broken.
Are you sure?
Whoop! That's an abscess all right!
Are you sure?
He's going to need to be hospitalized.
Are you sure?
It's a dog.
Are you sure?
All day long

*****

Nope. No problems! He just needs his shots. Why?
Well, either your dog has a sizable tumor or he's undergoing mitosis.

"I know I don't have an appointment, but why will I have to wait?"

ring ring ring ring ring

*****

"Doc! Come back quick! He's doin' that coughin' thing again!"

Ack! Ack!

You were closed Sunday, so I wasn't able to get his special food, forcing me to give him people food, which caused vomiting and diarrhea, so I had to take him to the emergency clinic! I'm sure you can see where this is your fault!

*****

We have a note in our computer that you prefer to see Dr. Scott.

phone: "It's not that we prefer Dr. Scott, it's just we hate him less than the others."

"Let me see if I understand you correctly. You're only _now_ seeking behavioral advice for problems that have been going on for twelve years?"

*****

There is an inverse relationship between the dedicatedness of the owner and the prognosis

"We'll spend whatever it takes!"

*****

Your dog is acting weird, because you're weird.

Clinic A - 1st visit

snap!

Clinic A - 2nd visit

If you really think he needs it.....

Rowr! Growl! *Grrrrr.....*

Clinic A - 3rd visit

And he's sedated too!

Growl! Roar! Gnash!

Clinic B - 1st visit

He's never acted that way before.

Rowf! Rowf! Grrrrrooowwll

Clinic C - 1st visit

The first clinic I took him to did something to him and he's been this way ever since.

Bark! Bark! Grooowll....!

Evolution of Denial

*****

Well, this has been a productive half-hour discussing what you're not going to do.

He's constipated.
Why do you think he's constipated?
You're supposed to tell me that!
I mean what are you seeing at home that makes you think he's constipated?
Well, I don't Know.
Has he been blah blah blah?
Yes.
After exam....
He's not constipated.
How do you Know?
blahblahblah reasons.
Are you sure? Because I Know he's constipated.

"He's been like this ever since that surgery you did on him!"

"What? From seven years ago?"

*****

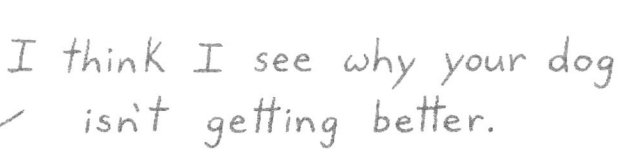

"I think I see why your dog isn't getting better."

OK, when I said he was depressed, I meant "clinically ill" or "lethargic", not sad.
YAY #1

*****

rrrrrrrr....
When owners state that they never see their pet licking at sutures

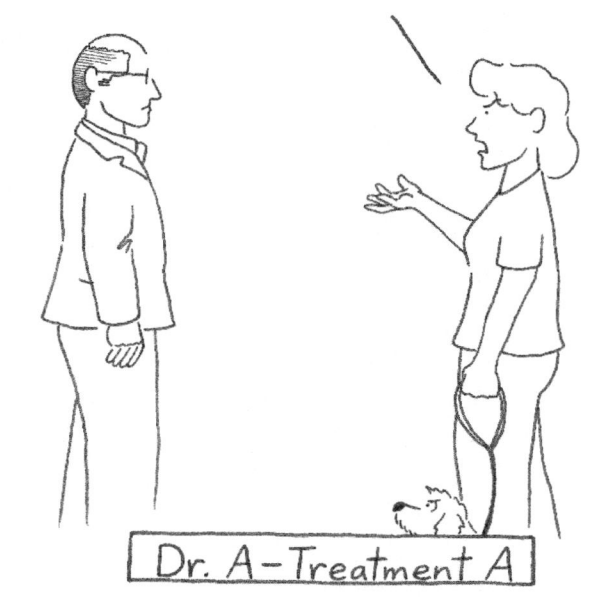

| What you tried didn't work at all! I'm going somewhere else! | What you recommended for Zeus really worked! You're the best! |

Dr. A – Treatment A | Dr. B – Treatment A

*****

No matter how much I talk I can't seem to get through.

Try this.

"I'm a nurse."

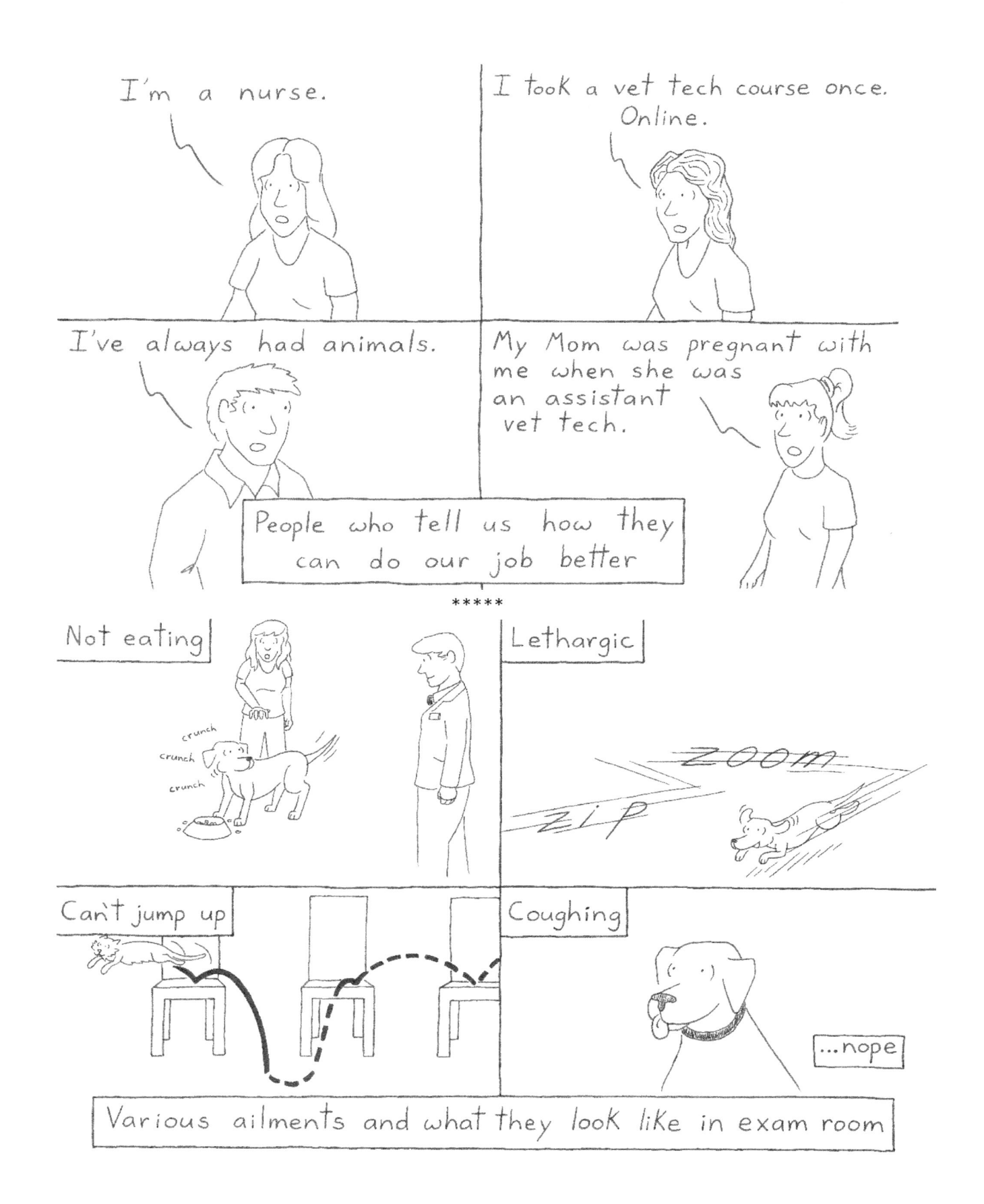

"I took a vet tech course once. Online."

"I've always had animals."

"My Mom was pregnant with me when she was an assistant vet tech."

People who tell us how they can do our job better

*****

Not eating
crunch crunch crunch

Lethargic
ZOOM ZIP

Can't jump up

Coughing
...nope

Various ailments and what they look like in exam room

blah blah blah
blah blah blah
blah blah
I can't afford to do that.
blah blah blah
blah blah
blah blah
blah
Oh, the reason that won't work is....
blah blah blah
blah blah blah
blah blah
blah
No, no. That's not possible because....
How else can I not help you today?

*****

What? Do you just pick medications at random?!
Oh, no. In school we're taught two main methods: "eenie meenie meinie mo" and "one potato, two potato."

Jun.: 15#	Jul.: 13#	Aug.: 12#	Sept.: 10#	Oct.: 9#
Nov.: 7#	Dec.: 5#	Jan.: 3.5#		

"Well, there's nothing we can do. I mean, see how bad he looks?"

*****

"Just because you don't agree, doesn't mean I'm wrong."

Has Max had this problem before?	My daughter's in the military.	You can start these tonight.	My cable is out.
He'll need strict rest after surgery.	I just got divorced.	How often are you giving the meds?	I like fish.

Non-Sequiturs

*****

When an owner declines everything, they can truthfully say for the rest of the pet's life:

We took him to the vet and he never got better.

"Do you have a doctor preference?"

"We prefer Dr. Scott because if we ignore anyone's advice, we want it to be his."

Clients As Children

I get a lot of push-back on this one, but I still think it's valid. It's also more of an observation than to provide advice on how to handle these situations. Again, I'm not talking about all clients here. If you keep this in mind, however, I think you'll find clients share a lot of behavior techniques with children.

Doubt me? Bring up neutering to a client who is averse to it. Watch their truculent body language, crossed arms, furrowed brow, ugly pout. Watch them shut down like a grade schooler being told they can't watch any more tv today. Explain how an owner can get urine from their cat at home by putting them for a time in a bathroom with an empty litterbox; the simplest of chores. It's like you've asked your teenager to clean their room for once. The wailing of "I can't do it!" or "That's too hard!" strikes that parent nerve in me like a gong. This goes for giving medication as well.

If you've been around kids at all, you'll find they all go through what I call their "lawyer" period. This is the time where they think everything is negotiable and will search out loopholes like a well-paid tax accountant. Semantics start to be very important to them, as well as nailing down time periods. As it is with clients. "I understand what the label said, but you didn't TELL me to give the medication!"

If you view providing prior medical or vaccine history from previous vets as homework assignments for clients, most fail in even this simple of tasks and with a similar litany of excuses that children use.

Another way they show juvenile tendencies is in how you can tell them not to do something and they just go ahead and do it anyway. With a child, it'll be something like, "Don't touch the stovetop, it's hot." Then they touch it and you're like, "I just told you not to do that!" With pet owners it'll be things like don't over-bathe your pet, don't feed people food, don't use hydrogen peroxide in the dog's ear, don't overfeed your pet, don't run them on your bike in hot weather, etc. etc. etc. One of my favorite ones was the third time a Boston terrier was brought in and hospitalized for pancreatitis because of being fed people food. The owners swore they would never do that again. A few weeks later I happened to run into them in public and they proudly told me, "We hardly ever give him people food anymore!" 'Hardly ever' is not zero. And no matter how much you harp on things they should do, such as flea or heartworm prevention, for example, your advice will go unheeded and as much as you'll feel compelled to when they have a flea problem or the dog comes up heartworm positive, you won't be able to tactfully say, "I told you so."

Clients, like children, tend to be selfish. They're only interested in their own needs and are not inclined to include others in their worldview, especially you or your staff. It's why they're consistently late (besides the implied disregard and disrespect it shows to our profession generally) and impatient to be seen regardless of other children needing to be attended to. I feel like telling them, "Santa only has one lap and no one likes the child who cuts in line."

One revealing characteristic is how they try to play the adults off each other. Mommy vet didn't give them the medication they wanted without a recheck? Well, they'll just see what Daddy vet has to say about that. He'll tell them "yes"! This goes for the strategy of using other parents (veterinary practices) to get what they want. "Where I used to go, Dr. Jones would let us get a refill without doing blood work!" sounds just as petulant as "Billy's Dad lets him stay up late!"

And I've also found the lovely tantrums displayed when an owner is told "no" are so very similar to denying my kids candy at the checkout counter. Had a client wanting a medication refill for a pet I hadn't seen for six months. He was told he needed to schedule a recheck appointment. As he hung up on my receptionist he said, "Tell the doctor, thanks for nothing!" To which I replied when I was told, "Aw. That's so sweet. He thanked me."

Whenever your child doesn't listen, try to remember this conversation, because I know where they got that behavior.

Money

One of the things I learned comparing my time in the Army with being a civilian vet is that when clients bring up money as an issue, that's not the issue. Yes, yes, yes, I know the argument that some people have legitimate financial restrictions and we need to be understanding of that. I'm not a monster. However, it is not my job and is completely beyond my ability to determine who can or cannot pay. My job is to recommend the best approach and then, if faced with an owner who can't or won't pursue diagnostics or treatments, try to tailor an approach that works for them and hopefully works for the health of the pet as well. What I have found though is people will object to almost any expenditure. Case in point: when I was in the Army, there was no exam fee, all procedures and medications were almost at cost, with barely a mark-up because the only thing that had to be paid for was a part-time civilian receptionist. Everything else, including surgery, equipment, rent, electricity, the technicians and veterinarian, everything, was paid for by Army funds. Think about that for a moment. Charges were miniscule. And people still complained about prices. That's why I don't have a lot of patience when it comes to this issue. It almost always strikes me as a bargaining tool and our practices are not some fold-up table at a flea market. I've found that the people who truly don't have funds will also not be the ones to express it or ask for a break or a discount. The ones that have the money but just don't want to part with it will be the negotiators or the deniers of care. I do things for free. I do give discounts. I sometimes don't charge for rechecks. Here's the difference. _I decide_ who I do it for. I don't get guilted or badgered into doing it. In fact, if that's a client's approach to me, even if I might have been initially inclined, it becomes a hard-no if they become pushy.

Another story is about an irate client who experienced "sticker shock" (their words), claiming that what she had done that day was wildly more expensive than when she had paid for similar services before. We brought up her receipts from the prior three years and there was only a modest increase over that time and were exactly what she had paid the previous year. She continued to argue the point since the facts did not fit her reality. She said she had a receipt at home and she was going to call back when she found it. She called back, all vindictive righteousness, and told me, based on this receipt, about the obvious price increases, validating her point. I asked, "What is the date on that receipt?" She was arguing from a nine-year-old receipt. When I pointed out that even gas and milk had increased over the past decade she, unwilling to accede ground, asked, "Can I expect for you to be raising your prices again, then?!" Yes, ma'am, most assuredly. Perhaps right after this phone call even.

The problem is not that veterinary care is expensive or even that the perception of value compared to cost is an issue. It's that there is a cost at all. While there is a tiny, itty-bitty, miniscule percentage of people who can and will spend money on their pets, the vast majority view maintenance issues or overt medical care as negotiable commodities. The oil change in the car is going to get precedence over a pet's care. I, too, have read the surveys where clients say their pet comes first and they'll pay whatever amount for their care. That survey is the way clients believe that they'll respond to a given abstract, future situation. When it gets down to actually parting with money, that is when the brakes will get applied. Clients don't appreciate or understand what it is we do. I believe it is not due to a lack on our part. I think the majority of us spend a great deal of time explaining things to clients, certainly more than our human medical counterparts. We're talking about clients who think being a veterinarian is a two-year degree (yes, I've been told this). Clients both overestimate what we make and underestimate how much things cost. Which is why we hear owners express "sticker shock", a self-induced delusional state. The cost of veterinary care is still an amazing deal. I've seen an article that asked, "Is the cost of care keeping clients away from your practice?" Well, maybe, but it's a trick question. It's not necessarily what you are charging, but what the clients are willing to part with. And what they're willing to part with is probably not going to keep you in business.

This means, Stop Worrying About What You're Charging! Sorry about that. I didn't mean to channel Samuel L. Jackson. I'm just tired of having money thrown in our faces as if we're some kind of greedy, upper 1% jerks. Not only do you see it in your clinic standing in front of you, but also in articles, client reviews, on the news, etc. It's this ubiquitous drumbeat placed in our brains that we're somehow responsible for other people's financial decisions. Understand, this is a tactic that clients use. Whether they are accusing you of being "all about the money" or they start listing all the other things that are impacting their lives, their own bills, medical maladies, children, disabled person they're taking care of, new house, oh how the list goes on. Often, they are just softening you up. Don't get me wrong. I'm not saying don't have a heart or don't feel for some of these people. Coming from a profession that carries so much debt load and being the lowest paid of the medical professions, we are definitely in a position to understand our clients. However, I'm pretty sure I'm not the only one who declines to use my personal problems and responsibilities to get people to give me discounts or to guilt my auto mechanic into giving me something free. I also don't understand how relaying financial woes to me changes what the cost of radiographs, medicine, or bloodwork is. They're able to do it or not do it; that's a conversation the clients need to have among themselves. I don't figure into it.

And we fall for this time and time again. We seem to be so fretful that we are "over-charging" clients. What does that mean? I charge a client for the work and product that is used. I charge no more or less than it takes to make a living, pay my own bills, pay staff, etc. etc. etc. You know the drill. None of us signed up to be monks and take a vow of poverty. "Over-charging" is a false construct. An "overcharge" would be something where you are charged more than you should have or for something that wasn't done. Which is what people are implying. Because they don't see the value in what we do or even in their pets' health. I have found that a client thinks something is "expensive" because it costs something. I suspect no other business gets hit up as often as we do for financial breaks and that's because animals are involved. We want to be liked. We want to see animals cared for. And people take advantage of those tendencies. Look, if you give discounts and breaks and don't charge people, it's ok. Just don't do it because of guilt. Don't beat yourself up or put yourself into financial straits (if you're not there already) because of not charging for what you do. Clients are people and people manipulate. Especially when it comes to money. I would venture to say that there isn't one veterinarian out there who actually gets paid what they're worth. We already sacrifice as it is.

I had a client whose dog was having inappropriate urination and I had asked her to bring in urine so we could do a urinalysis. It revealed a urinary tract infection. She was okay with paying for medication, but the client balked at paying for urinalysis. Her "logic"? Because I had *asked* for her to bring urine in, she was doing *me* a favor, therefore she shouldn't be charged.

People complain. People yell. But, ultimately, it's not really about money. It's about getting something for free or less. I think it's more accurate to accuse a client of being "all about the money". I don't actually make a big deal out of what we charge at our clinic. The client does. I hate talking about money. Clients love talking about money. "How much is this?" "How much is that?" "Why is that so much?" "Can I get this cheaper elsewhere?" For me I don't get invested (see what I did there?) in a client's financial decision-making process. I present the charge or estimate. They tell me whether they want to proceed or not. In those few times I actually look at the bottom-line of an estimate, I'm always amazed at how relatively inexpensive it is for what we're doing. Feel free to compare costs and efficiency with any other medical profession. I knew someone who had their gall bladder removed endoscopically back in the early-90s. No insurance. A bit over $10,000. Same cost in a similar sized dog? Probably less than $1000.

If pet insurance, third-party credit, or credit cards are not enough payment options, I'm not sure where it becomes yet another responsibility on us to be financial consultants as well. I am tired of literally and figuratively "discounting" our profession. Set up how you want to practice and how you offer things and price according to the realities of your facility, financial obligations, and level of medicine. Do this knowing it will not satisfy everyone. None of us are required to suit and assuage everyone. We try to be everything to everyone and make it so we live in a world where never is heard a discouraging word. The prices are what the prices are. I don't dispute with my car mechanic or dentist what they charge. I don't apologize, either, for charging for the services we provide. I have commiserated with owners over costs. I, too, can not afford anything and everything.

When a client says they don't have any money, often they mean that they have money, just not for the things you're advising. As one eloquent client put it to me, "Well, Doc, if I pay you, how am I gonna afford my cigarettes and booze?" How would you reply to this? Personally, I've found no amount of logic or pleading will change a client's mind. Our job is to advise. The client's job is to do what you advise, but it is no fault of yours if a client declines to do their part. I find a lot of us are really hard on ourselves in these situations. If we just say the right words, in the right magical way, a client will see the light and comprehend the importance of treating. But, we're only one part of the communication pathway. We cannot shoulder the burden that justly falls on another's shoulders. I resent when an owner tries to put responsibility on me that is rightly theirs. Recognize when this is happening. We cannot care more than the clients. We will. But we can't. And clients will frustrate you. It's exhausting to the body and draining of the emotions if we allow our empathy full control. We have to take a step back, which is completely against everything we've ever done to get to this point. It's protective. It's one of the dichotomies we have to balance, that of wanting to take care of the animal and feeling like we have to make it as inexpensive as possible for an owner and still keep the lights on and the staff paid. The veterinary profession is a marathon; it's not a sprint. Runners will tell you there is a different training process between these two approaches. The mind-set in practice is like a cross-country, hiliathlon (that's a thousand-event contest I just made up). You have to pace yourself if you want that endorphin high and wish to reach the finish line. You have to pick your battles. You cannot go home with clients and do the insulin injections for them. The neediness of owners is boundless and your own resources, both physical and emotional are limited.

Tempering expectations helps. We have expectations all through our path to getting to be a veterinarian. Many of us are disappointed upon arrival. Our expectations have to get down-sized or changed. The same goes for client compliance. Do your part. Advise, educate, request follow-ups, do call-backs, etc. Certainly, hope the client does their part. However, be prepared for them not to as well.

Your best choice is option A which is.....

Option B doesn't help us all the way, however....

Option C is.....

I'm just going to ignore it.

Ah! That would be option D.

*****

Oh, I won't be able to pay that. I don't have any cash, checks, or credit cards. But, everything was tasty.

My hair feels great. Thanks! I'll come back in and pay you on Friday after I get paid.

Barb's Hairstyles

Thanks for rebuilding my car's engine, but I only have $20.

Let me take these home and I'll come back and pay.

Clients in other situations

128

What's wrong with the dog?

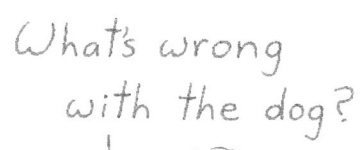

I don't know. The client suffers from hypomoneyia.

*****

For three days of hospitalized treatment it will be about $500. More conservative treatment will be about $250.

Is there anything we can do that's cheaper?

Well, sub-Q fluids is $30, anti-vomiting meds $20, antibiotics about $25, and prayer is free.

"There should be a wing of the hospital named after me for all of the money I've spent here!"

"With all of the money you've spent here, we had your name engraved on the toilet bowl handle to remind us daily of your worth."

*****

"I didn't like your attitude!"

"I can't believe you would charge me for a follow-up when it was **your** antibiotics that didn't work!"

"I didn't agree with what you said!"

"But, it's a stray and not even mine!"

Client Logic: Reasons Not to Pay

"Can I just pay half now?"

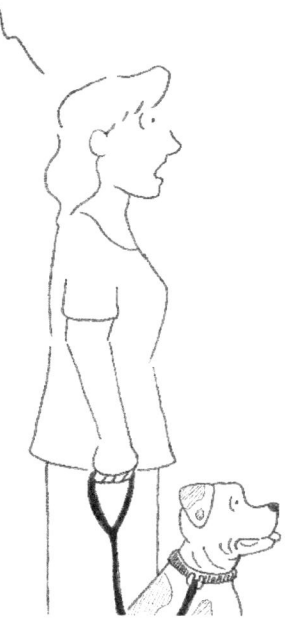

"Sure! I'll give you half the diagnosis now and the other half when you pay in full!"

*****

"Mr. Jones just walked in. He wants you to come out to the lobby and take, as he said, 'a quick look at my dog.'"

"Quick look? Sure!"

"What do you think it is, Doc?"

"Oh. Sorry. 'Looking' is free. An opinion's gonna cost you."

Veterinary Medicine: 3022 AD

> How much is this gonna cost, Doc?

*****

> You're just in it for the money!

> That's not true. I also do it for the respect and admiration I get from the public.

"Certainly at ten years old there are a number of things that could be wrong. We should do bloodwork, possibly x-rays."

"You know what? He's really nineteen. They must have his age wrong. He's much too old to put him through all that."

*****

"The owner said they're not going to treat. They're just going to take the estimate you gave them and rub it on the problem twice a day until it gets better."

134

We knew finances were an issue, so we didn't charge for the extra day of hospitalization, the last antibiotic injection, and the subQ fluids before sending him home.

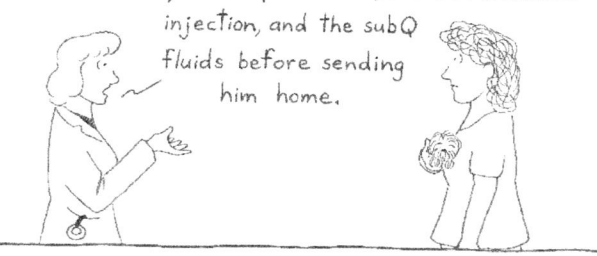

Why would you charge? That would have been over the estimate!

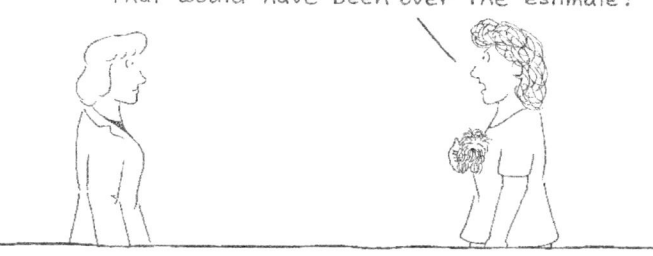

In your language that must mean "Thank you."

*****

I'm on a fixed income.

Well, I'm on a broke income. At least yours is fixed.

"Money is not a problem."

...because I don't plan on paying anyway.

*****

"Now, get me a diagnosis!"

How I feel sometimes working within a client's constraints

How clients seem to think we should live so we don't look like we're in it for the money.

I bet what I spent at your clinic paid for that nice, comfy rock!

*****

Come on, hypocalcemia! Because that's the only diagnosis the client can afford!

buzz buzz   whirrrrr

Are they going to do anything?

The only thing productive in that room was the dog's cough.

*****

I'm so glad I switched clinics. My last vet charged for *everything!*

"A spay is that much?! How much is it without anesthesia?"

*****

I realize it's difficult to know whether to treat or not, especially when costs are a consideration.

"I can't afford to do anything, so what can you do for me?"

*****

"I'm not happy! I've spent $500 here and I'm not satisfied!"

"Well, ma'am, I'm a veterinarian, not a gigolo."

Hi! I'm.....

I'm on disability! My husband was laid off! My son is handicapped and we're still paying on his surgery from last year! Our house was flooded and we're living in a motel! My check doesn't come in for two weeks! The car!

.... Dr. Scott.

*****

VETERINARIAN HELP 5¢

THE DOCTOR IS [IN]

I ONLY HAVE TWO CENTS. WHAT CAN YOU DO FOR ME?

Thanks Sparky!

We're going to run a CBC and chem panel. We'll start fluids and antibiotics. This virus can kill him in 24 hours if we don't. It will cost about $400 over three days.

blah... blah... blah....blah ...blah... blah blah...blah.... blahbity blah.... blah.... blah.... blahblahblah....blah .... blah $400... blah blah

Why so much?

Klunk

What veterinarians say

What clients hear

*****

Is that you're best guess?

No, that was my second best. For my *best* guess you have to pay more.

Insults

Let's just get this out of the way up front:

"You don't care about animals."

"All you care about is money."

"If you really cared, you'd help me out."

"You're just going to let my pet die."

"You're just a licensed pet killer."

"You're holding my pet hostage." (this one is usually stated when either payment is insisted upon before turning the pet over to the client after hospitalization and/or surgery or when, though you've given plenty of prior warning, you refuse to refill medication until the owner brings the pet in for a recheck or for follow-up bloodwork; this latter situation will sometimes include the statement, "I'll guess you'll just let him die then" or "when he dies, I'll lay his body on your doorstep", neither of which has ever happened, by the way)

These are only a small fraction of the hurtful things that owners have thrown my way. I've been called a "butcher" in regards to a surgery I performed. I've been called "smug" and "smirky" and "rude". I've been told I "take advantage of concerned pet owners". I've been told I "price-gouge". I'm the "worst vet" they've ever met. The ones who call me the worst vet ever, without any caveat, I ask, "Have you met every vet in the world?"

None of these are true, of course. Sadly, I'm sure my list of insults (that I can remember, because my brain has a self-defense mechanism that flushes a lot of these out the back of my cerebellum) pales in comparison to what others in the veterinary profession have had laid at their feet. These are hateful, grade-school level taunts meant to hurt and illicit a negative response from the designated recipient. I find them trite and unoriginal. I couldn't wait to become an adult because I thought it would be a step up and away from the bullying, harassment, and belittling I received as a child from other kids. Little did I know that it carries on into adulthood and petty people just put an adult justification, a fresh veneer, on their small-mindedness. I easily identify these people and reject their hurtful premises because I have unfortunately had too much experience in this particular coliseum. I was lucky to already have a thick skin and know who I am apart from other peoples' incorrect summaries when I started this job. I bring these situations up here so others don't get caught off-guard. Did anyone ever think that when they were heading into this profession that these would be some of the things we would have to put up with? I don't think so.

I've been given advice that words can only hurt if you let them. While I think there is some truth in that, they still hurt. Especially in the sheer volume and frequency of people who feel that it is perfectly fine to verbally abuse others. It's like death by a thousand cuts. Early in a career, you can't help but take it personally and feel you've done something wrong if you haven't been prepared to look for it when it happens. It's just one of those things that isn't discussed and therefore most of us are left defenseless. It's not an "if" it will happen, it's a matter of "when".

After twenty-plus years, I have built up a considerable amount of protective psychic scarring. It's a by-product of any job where you deal with the public, where you deal with illness, death, and people. We are a well-meaning and conscientious lot who can be easily hurt and I don't think we do a good job protecting each other. Being forewarned that people are going to say these things will hopefully allow you to put them into context. Because when they use these demeaning words, it's not really about you, it's about them and their approach to life. There's only one person whose standards you have to live up to. And that person is you. You know that those slurs aren't true and that is all that matters. They may go to their friends, another vet, on-line, and tell these untruths. You can't control people. Many of them are assholes with poor sphincter control. As difficult as it is, you can't let it damage you. You know the truth. Do others think badly of me because of the way I've been depicted through another person's lens? Yes, probably. Do I care? No, not really. Can I change their viewpoint? Maybe, but I'm not going to be given the chance to, because these people won't be brave enough to bring it up directly to me. And if they do, I can tell them my version, but I'm also not going to plead with them to believe me. Am I going to devote any time to tracking down everywhere I have been verbally maligned by others? Nope. Not at all. I don't have that kind of time or energy into convincing people of my veracity and good-nature. I have literally left behind caring when people go off on me. I find these encounters boring, something to endure and get through. Their juvenile jibes are the adult equivalent of being called "Four Eyes" in third grade. I just wish they'd be more creative, so I could at least say, "Hey, that was a good one! I haven't heard that one before!" Sadly, we need to become adept at identifying bullying behavior to do our job. Our first instinct is to wonder what we could have done wrong to warrant such venom from people, but I've found it's not us, it's them. They can like me or not like me. I know I'm a good person and that's all that matters at the end of the day.

An example: I heard of a technician who was berated for having missed clipping a toenail. Now, understand, this "oversight", wasn't brought up right away. It was brought up two months later, so please bring your skepticism. This owner didn't feel it was sufficient to just let her know. She had to go on to say how disappointed she was and she couldn't believe she had still been charged and she expected better of this technician. Even with an apology and a question as to why she just didn't come back and let her clip the "missed" toenail, this client continued to heap condemnation on her. This is bullying behavior aimed at putting someone into a position of trying to please more and more a person who will never be pleased.

This can be seen also with what I call "Gotcha!" behavior. This can happen in several scenarios. One is when an owner is seeking a second opinion and won't share anything about what the first opinion was or what diagnostics were done to, as I've been told by them, "keep you honest". Which reminds me of the one client who obliviously stated, "Your second opinion just agrees with the first opinion I got! What good does that do me?!" Owners will withhold information until you start making observations or suggestions then think they "Gotcha!" because you hadn't considered something, but you would have if you'd had all the facts. I've had owners let me do a full physical while professing the pet had exhibited no problems and when I've confirmed the pet seems healthy they suddenly ask why I hadn't noticed his lameness or what they considered a bloated belly. Well, probably because he didn't show any signs during my physical and you gave me no indication you had concerns of perception of your own for me to elaborate on during my exam. Another example is when a client believes they've been told something incorrectly when usually it is a misinterpretation on their part, but they want to use this perceived oversight to hector us and our staff. I'm not sure why people engage in this activity as it truly benefits no one.

I have heard from others who have been told by their bosses to just suck it up and take such abuse because, after all, the client is paying them. This is reprehensible. None of us are servants. None of us need ever put up with such tactics from anyone, I don't care how much money they throw our way. Your value as a person is much greater than any monetary compensation. Bowing and scraping are not services we provide. Negative behavior toward staff members should not be tolerated by veterinary owners. What? You're worried you're going to lose business? You don't care as long as it's not you being yelled at? You're worried they're going to write a bad review? Let them! When we allow these things, or god forbid reward them, we are just creating more terrible encounters in the future. We should not be engendering abusive relationships with our clientele. I think many people feel it's ok to say the things they do because they don't think we will fight back, because we're locked into this social context of being the better person, being the rational, reasonable one. We can still be that, but stand firm in the face of their accusations. There's a saying about boyfriends I've heard that relates to client situations like these: "If your boyfriend is nice to you, but not nice to the food server, they are not a nice person." You know you have clients that abuse everyone on the staff, but put on a different face with the doctor. We should not tolerate abusive relationships; our self-worth is more important. The more we all push back against this kind of verbal tyranny, the more we set up proper modes of communication and interaction, the less we should see these things occur. Notice I said "less" not "end". Unfortunately, there will always be jerks in the world.

Reviews

We seem to be a profession made up of schizophrenics. You're going to find that reviews will paint you as a saint or as the "worst person to walk the face of the earth" as one review says. Neither are true. There is really never any middle ground or constructive criticism given. I find 99.99% of negative reviews to be fiction, bordering on fantasy; a false narrative delicately strung along tenuous points of truth. Negative reviews are meant to hurt and also depict the client writing them as a victim. Some people advocate telling your side of the story and being professional in your response. I'm not one of those people. Responding to negative reviews rewards the client writing. They know they got to you. And the problem in these situations is it's an emotional issue and being reasonable and polite will almost always lose to vehemence and vitriol. It becomes a they said/they said interminable contest.

I don't respond to them. There may be credence to playing to an audience who will see your response and weigh it in considering who is right or wrong in a situation. I do believe this feeling like we're on trial with every case we touch hovers at the back of our brains. And people wonder why we get defensive. You'll have just as many people who think the client review is bogus as those reading your response being just so much damage control and "of course the vet will deny everything". There are better ways to spend your time. I read my negative reviews when I wish to see how people mangle logic and the chronology of events. I find amusement in the things people say about me. Plus I enjoy fiction.

This critiquing and animosity toward our profession has always been around. It's just that the internet and social media augments it. In the past people would also get angry at their vet. They were just limited in their sphere; telling their neighbor, friends, family what a terrible experience they had. If there's one thing I'd like to convey to you is you have little ability to change someone's mind about you or the stories they may tell. If you feel the need to defend yourself, do so. Just be aware that the only important person in the equation is you. Not what the client thinks. Not what their friends and fellow bloggers think, the tangential people who seem to have some personal stake in a situation of which they weren't even part. Just you. As long as you know the truth and know you did the best job you could, that is what is important. Words hurt. No doubt. But trolls win if they infect us with doubt and we let those wounds fester.

This is why I don't respond to negative reviews. They're superfluous to how I view myself. I don't care if others dislike me because of whatever falsehoods they've heard about me. I don't have the time and energy to run around and explain and defend myself to everyone. We need to have the self-esteem to brush these criticisms off. I'm not saying it's easy, but it will happen even to the best, brightest, and well-intentioned of us. I'm telling you now, don't fall for the trap.

Worrying about reviews, either past or future, will also affect your everyday life if you allow it. Educate, document things as best as possible, give advice, empathy, and understanding to the best of your ability. And you'll still get negative reviews at times. It is just what people do. Don't take it personally. I've even joked with my staff. "Hey! Did you know I suck?"

I don't want to bad-mouth our last vet.

But.......

sigh

"I'm never coming back here again!"

"Promise?"

*****

"I read your reviews and I have to say, you're not the rude, uncaring A-holes running a dirty, smelly rat den that I'd been led to believe!"

Divorce Letters

I bring this up because I hear a lot of angst over this issue. And I don't understand it. Because if your thoughts have arrived at even whether you should divorce a client from the practice or not, the answer is "yes". I know the level of trouble we have to deal with on an average day, with an average client, and it's pretty high. We have a pretty low bar when it comes to our expectations of clients. And we have an equally high threshold of pain for behaviors that we tolerate. There's a lot of run-of-the-mill abuse and complaining that we just take as a matter-of-course in a day. Therefore, if a client stands out from that already high level of tolerance, they've earned a divorce letter.

Swearing at staff is an automatic divorce letter. Consistent ignoring or dismissal of medical recommendations? Divorce letter. There are many shades of grey, but I'll state again, if you're thinking about it, you're probably right to do so. If an owner has told you they aren't returning, make sure they get a letter as well, because people can be notorious liars and I've had these bad pennies turn back up on our doorstep time and time again. The divorce letter just emphasizes that, yes, that's right, we concur you won't be coming back here.

A lot of worry is whether it will cause more problems or not. Yeah, it might. But so might the continued presence of this toxic person in your practice. Some fret over wording. I say keep it simple. You don't have to explain yourself. Just tell them the generalities, you will no longer see them or their pets, and you'll send their paperwork to whatever practice they decide to go to next. I enjoy writing divorce letters, personally. It's very cathartic. And, it may surprise you, I haven't done that many in all these years. Again, probably because we put up with more than we should. It also assures me, however, that when it is time, these folks have really gone out of their way to be difficult.

For your amusement, I've included a divorce letter that I wrote up once (I don't remember the circumstances) but did not send in this form. It may be therapeutic to write a letter like this, venting things the way you'd like to before composing the firm and politer one. If you're worried you're being too harsh toward a client in the wording of your divorce letter, I think it's safe to say as long as you are politer than this letter below, you're probably fine.

Here it is:

""We understand, per our last conversation, that you will no longer be using our services. We wanted to make sure that you understand that this letter was already in process before you made this decision. You were consistently rude, inconsiderate, and uncooperative with every staff member from the moment you walked in our door. And this is ignoring the fact that you created an uncomfortable and problematic situation when you were unable to pay for services when rendered - a rather normal and understood concept that should require no explanation to a functioning adult. It became obvious to us that we would not be able to fulfill your needs and therefore recommend you find another veterinarian to ensure care for your pets. We will supply updated medical records to the veterinary facility you choose.

On a personal note, I am sorry that either through genetics or a number of tragic events in your life that you have such a jaundiced soul your self-hate oozes out like an infected sore onto everyone you come into contact with. I have truly never met such a nasty individual as yourself and suspect that Mother Theresa would shun you. I also feel sorry for the veterinary facility that you choose next to go to, though I am glad that you have the companionship of animals that have the inability to distinguish good behavior from bad. It is remarkable that someone with the abrasive characteristics of 40 grit sandpaper can still find employment, even if it be amongst the felonious and incarcerated. May you eventually rest in peace."

Judging

In different formats, I keep running across a common exhortation to not judge clients. Enough so that it's started to make my conspiratorial mind think these are directed specifically at me. Well, here's the thing, I do judge clients. When the client says he's not going to do anything about a perfectly operable mass that is very concerning because, "after all, Doc, he's just a dog and frankly he's not worth it", yeah, I am judging that client. When a client wants to talk euthanasia because their cat has been peeing in the house and has a curable urinary tract infection, yeah, I am judging that client. When a client tells me that they are going to or have just come back from an extravagant vacation and therefore aren't going to treat what is a relatively inexpensive problem because of said vacation, I am silently judging. I have another client who, if you first met him, you would think he is a homeless alcoholic. His dog has multiple problems. Yet, he does everything I recommend and does an admirable job of compliance. I judge him too, just this time in a favorable way.

I am not a saint. I judge. And if we're being honest, so does everyone reading these words. Here's the thing, and what I think people are really trying to say, don't let your judgment of a client's presumed economic status interfere in your recommendations or care of their pet. If they seem poorer, don't automatically alter your first recommendation lower. Conversely, if they seem richer, don't automatically ratchet up your recommendation because you figure they'll go for it and pay for anything. Make your best recommendation and go from there. I do think we need to re-tailor an initial recommendation depending on what the owner can or is willing to do. After all, when we talk to clients, it's all negotiation as far as they're concerned. I think we can sometimes be obstinate in insisting on only the best recommendation, though there are situations where that truly is the only choice. However, I am often presented with having to offer alternatives for various reasons and that's fine. As well as common. They always get my best initially though.

I have found people who don't want to care for their pet crosses the entire range of socioeconomic status. I have had people scrimp and scrape and borrow to get their pet taken care of. I have had people, who are decidedly wealthier than I can ever expect to be, reject the simplest of diagnostics due to expense. Well, they expressed that it was due to expense, though it was really due to not caring enough. Yes, I judged them. I also judged those people who seemed to ardently care for their pet and were trying to do right within their limited means. Those people I try to help out and I do more for them from a financial stand-point because of that positive judgment. The people who express the tragedy of their lives as part of an initial negotiation don't get a lot from me, because I recognize that as a gambit and not a real need on their part. They're just bringing those things up to get me to do less or to discount costs. I find that the people who have true need don't pull that gambit. You can tell the difference between the two, especially the longer you're in this career.

Here's the funny thing. Clients judge us all the time. And I get misjudged a lot. I work at two places. One is my regular clinic where I am part owner. The other place I am paid as an hourly employee if you will. I get judged as being more honest at the second place because clients don't view me as "in it for the money", as far as recommendations go. I want to tell them, well I actually am in it for the money, because if they didn't pay me, I wouldn't be there. At my own clinic, recommendations are looked at askance as to whether they are "really necessary" or just so I can "build that new wing" and name it after a client. I make the same recommendations regardless of where I am. I don't get hung-up on this issue though because that's just people and I have found I just can't control them and their perceptions.

So, yes, we judge people. Just don't do it in such a way that you look at a client and then offer recommendations higher or lower than you would for anyone else. I treat everyone the same way, or I like to think I do. I often know when I make a recommendation whether the person in front of me is going to decline. I still make it. And sometimes I get pleasantly surprised. Here's a promise. I will stop judging clients when they stop judging me.

Euthanasia

It's assumed by a lot of our clients that euthanasia is the worst part of our job. And, certainly, I'm not one to deny to them that it is certainly "one" of the harder parts of our job. Because, you know, it's not considered diplomatic to say that the worst part of our job is dealing with people. And, while difficult, I don't consider euthanasia a bad thing. More often than not I think it is the last, nice thing we can do for our friends. I'm glad we have the option, since the alternative is to just let them go on, a slow slide of deterioration. I'd like to present some other aspects of euthanasia that you may or may not be aware of, depending how long you've been practicing.

Euthanasia by estimate. There are times we can put a dollar value on a problem that overwhelms a client. They stop thinking. Especially if it is presented as "do the estimate or euthanize, there is no middle ground". As a general practitioner, we are rarely able to do anything and everything. Often, we are forced, usually by client financial constraints, to do supportive or symptomatic therapy in the face of an unknown problem. While we provide the best options, clients rarely pick up that baton when it's passed. We have to be able to offer alternatives to a black and white estimate, where we can, even if all it does is palliative care.

I believe most pets live a "financial life-span". This is one of those unspoken, unfortunate burdens we have to bear. Weighing options and prioritizing tests is one of those things they don't prepare us well for in vet school. We are made to believe that we, and the client, will pursue every option possible. This is just not so. We find we have to be careful, therefore, in considering the concept of a financial life-span, that we don't inadvertently induce euthanasia by estimate.

If we feel we can help the pet at all by doing less, giving comfort or hopefully getting over the crest of an emergent disease, we should. Also, if we provided no alternative, many clients will feel compelled to euthanize rather than do what is in the estimate. We need to be cognizant of how estimates are viewed by clients. As an aside, I've found that most clients have a three-test limit. They may be ok with things right up until that fourth test is needed, then they start feeling like there's no end to the testing. Others think they're a contestant on the "Name That Disease" game show and try to get a diagnosis with "just one test"!

Holiday euthanasia. This one may seem obvious to a lot of us. I don't think that pets are timing their decline to coincide with holidays. I think what is happening is that clients will often have family visiting and they start assigning greater problems to their pets. Not deliberately, not malignly, not even, I think, with the intention to decide on euthanasia. They just start looking at the things that they've accepted in a declining pet through the eyes of visiting family and those things start to look worse. Also, many people would rather make the decision pre-holiday because they convince themselves how awful it would be if their pet passed away during the holiday. The follow-up aspect to this is that a new pet can be introduced during the holidays to assuage the loss of the previous pet. Sounds cold and calculated, but I don't think it's meant that way.

Euthanasia by reminder card. I've seen this time and time again and it is similar to the holiday way of thinking. What happens sometimes when we send a friendly reminder card for vaccines or heartworm test, etc. is the unintended consequence that a client starts viewing whether they want to continue investing money into the pet. It's an unfortunate mental calculus that a lot of people go through in making these decisions. The things that they have been doing or putting up with or maintaining with medication, instead of being just the day to day routine, now becomes a decision-making process brought on by a reminder card. Not to suggest we stop sending reminder cards, but when euthanasia is brought up, just glance to see if the pet is due for anything that you've sent a reminder out recently. You might find it enlightening.

Withdrawal of care euthanasia. This is an odd one. And I have to think it's a normal human behavior, because I've seen it a lot and I don't think people are always doing this deliberately. These are cases where there has been a long-term treatment process, such as heart disease. The owners have been compliant for a long time and the pet has been doing well. Suddenly the pet is in decline and presented for euthanasia. And what you'll sometimes find when reviewing the chart is that the owners stopped refilling medication. Therefore, the pet gets worse. And the clients seem truthfully oblivious to the fact that they haven't been giving the medication as diligently as usual and as prescribed. Again, I don't think this is deliberate. I think there might be subconscious behavior going on that in withdrawing care, the pet gets worse, the clients can now feel ok to make a euthanasia decision, because, after all, "see how bad they look".

This isn't really a section with answers. Just some things I've noticed over the years and I've not seen them brought up in other venues. I think it's good to be aware of these types of behaviors and recognize them when they occur. It may give you insight into which way to direct a conversation with a client. Or, at least, give you a better understanding into how our fellow primates operate.

Convenience Euthanasia

How do you define convenience euthanasia? And do you perform convenience euthanasias? I ask, because I've found we don't all agree on where that line is drawn. Let me start where I define it. For me a convenience euthanasia is a healthy pet or one who has a small but easily surmountable problem (ie urinary tract infection) that an owner just wants put down for some reason (they're moving, they just don't want to put up with it, it can't possibly go live with someone else, they've tried finding it a home but couldn't - I mean, really, the list of excuses is endless). I don't euthanize these pets. And I've had people angry with me about it. I just tell them that I have to be able to sleep well at night and that I'm sure that they can find someone to perform the euthanasia, but it won't be me. Nothing like being yelled at for *not* euthanizing a healthy animal.

Some in our profession seem to define convenience euthanasia as euthanizing anything that is fixable, no matter how difficult. Here's where I think we enter murky territory, because we deal with many more of these types of cases than the type handed to us in the first paragraph. Say there's a newly diabetic pet and the owner just does not have the time, schedule, finances, or ability to care for it in a proper manner. You know, untreated, it's going to go downhill and probably in an ugly way. Is euthanasia a convenience or a necessity in this circumstance? If I am presented with a situation like this, I'm not going to like it, but, yes, I will euthanize since the alternative is for the pet to get no care and do poorly. For the owner, the disease they are presented with may be inconvenient and they're making decisions based on that, but, for me, I look at it as the unfortunate best thing I can do for the pet second to treating.

When I am presented chronic conditions, I sometimes have to go through this thought process. I've had just terrible skin conditions presented to me for the first time with no prior treatment history (and what prompted the owner to suddenly seek care, what level of problem became so terrible it bothered even their low sensibilities is usually unclear) and you can just tell that the pet has had a hard and awful life and will continue to do so in the future in the hands of these people even if you could convince them to treat. These are conditions that have a steep hill, but could be made better through effort. Again, however, if the owner is unwilling/unable to do so, I have euthanized these pets as a mercy. At a minimum, I feel I have at least taken them out of their ongoing chronic suffering and misery.

Now, many of us take the tact of having owners relinquish pets in some of these circumstances that I'm bringing up. That is certainly a valid choice. I will admit that I don't go down that road, because it just seems like a never-ending spiral. There are just so many (too many) cases where you just know you can fix it, yet are denied the opportunity.

It's often better when we have had a manageable case (Cushing's, age-related ailments, renal, etc.) that the owner has done everything they could but eventually starts getting negative returns, as none of us can keep things going on forever. In these cases, I think we all agree there's a time where euthanasia is more than justified, even if that exact right moment isn't clear to any of us. These we can at least countenance it as part of the life process and feel validated in helping the pet out.

It's those other grey areas we have to define for ourselves where euthanasia is proper and where we are doing it just because the owner wants it. I don't have the right answer, just the right answer for me. Even with my standards there have been times that I anguished over whether I made the right decision for the pet. Could have, would have, should have are often the worst questions for us. Sometimes I've felt that I've had to trust an owner's story or perception as to the extent of a patient's problem as seen in the home setting. And I don't trust lightly. I have euthanized some pets where I was doubtful as to the veracity of the owner's story, but also felt, if true, euthanasia would be an option. Were these convenience euthanasias? I don't know. Possibly only the owners do.

This is one of the conversations, one of these uncertainties of life that weigh upon us. We can really only answer the question on a case by case basis. And we just need to make sure we answer the question based on our comfort level, not the owner's. I am more than willing to be yelled at for not euthanizing an animal if I feel it is unwarranted. Because, ultimately, we are there for the pets, not the owners, even if they may think otherwise.

"So, what is Toby in for?"

"Well, we're either going to euthanize him or get a nail trim."

*****

"Let me summarize — he has many problems that you've done nothing about, but that have now led you to choose euthanasia."

How far do you go in describing what might happen during a euthanasia?

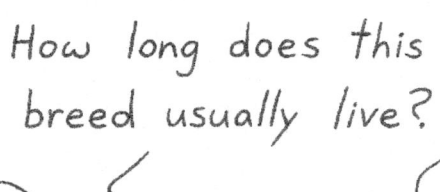

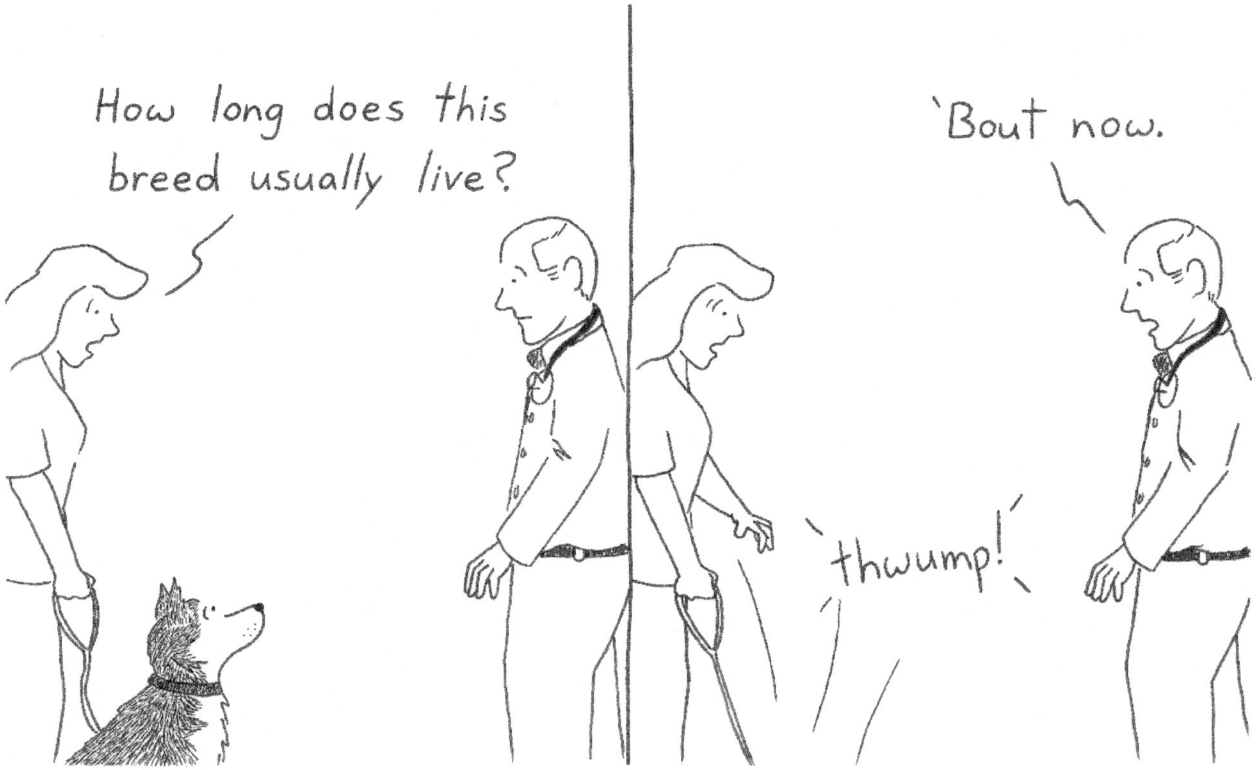

How long does this breed usually live?

'Bout now.

thwump!

*****

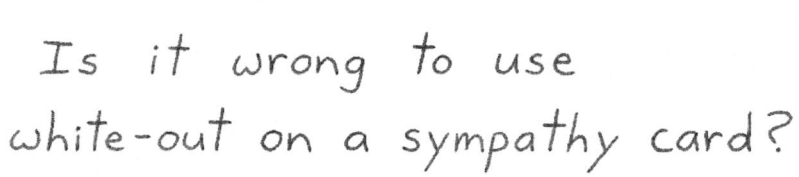

Is it wrong to use white-out on a sympathy card?

Products That Kill (Spoiler: they all kill)

Just for fun, take the name of any veterinary product from the last fifteen years, go to the Google and put in (product name) and then the word "kills". Now, granted, you're not going to find that everything kills, but you'll find websites, blogs, rantings and ravings about the evils of any of these products. Anything from anti-inflammatories to injectable heartworm medication to flea preventions (both oral and topical), urinary sphincter meds, etc. you can find someone with a lot of time on their hands who is running a crusade to get these products off the market. And they are rife with misinformation or incomplete and skewed information. You can, if you want to waste some time, even generically put in things such as antibiotics and vaccines and see who's against those. Besides specific stories that people have, and you'll find one pet's story is told multiple times so that it looks like a bigger problem than just the one alleged incident, they also rail against the host of side-effects these drugs have, as if there's no reason to be giving these medications other than to cause harm to the animals. I joked with the sales reps of a new flea medication that was just released how long it would take for someone to start up a campaign against it, because anything new is obviously bad. Ironically, anything old seems to be good, with people touting ancient 12th Century Chinese herbs (and, no, please don't send me notes about how you know these things work and why; it's not that I'm close-minded or not informed – I've done my due diligence and like the products above, I'm not picking specifically on ancient Chinese secrets like Calgon) and colloidal silver because not only do they work, but, hey, no negative side-effects! And aren't all side-effects considered negative? Some people don't want to give their pets "poisons" or "over-medicate" them with flea or heartworm preventatives, without considering that getting fleas and heartworm cause side-effects all on their own. I've had some people not want to vaccinate their pets, as if parvo and feline leukemia didn't have some very serious down-sides. I sometimes want to ask these folks, "So, you must not drive a car. Oh, you do? Well, that's odd, because the likelihood of having an accident is much higher than if you walk everywhere you need to go. What, with your concern for repercussions, if you weren't here standing in front of me, I'd assume you probably don't leave the house either. And I've seen you drive; there are some potentially serious side-effects both to you and others."

People will take all sorts of medications themselves, it's a veritable pharmapalooza at your local WaltMart, without the direction of a physician, with perhaps dubious reasoning for taking them, and perhaps even mixing medications that shouldn't be, all without once thinking of potential side-effects or cross-effects. If you point out that you can look up and find the side-effects from something as ubiquitous as aspirin, you'll get a blank stare from clients, because, well, aspirin has been around for long enough to not generate anxiety. However, for some reason, we dispense a new product and there are people out there waiting to jump on it like a cockroach on a kitchen crumb. As far as I can tell, anything new is bad and has unacceptable side-effects and anything old really, really works and has no side-effects. Well, intellectually, this just can't be. I'm not sure how, in the 21st century, people seem surprised that there might be side-effects to a medication. Even the allergy, penile dysfunction, and allergy to penile dysfunction medications on television ads have the Voice-Over of Doom intoning how your spleen can explode and amorous bees may be attracted to your scent as possible side-effects.

So, I submit the following that you can feel free to use the next time you have someone who's angry that you would dare to give them something to help their pet that has potential side-effects, whether their pet is actually exhibiting any or not.

Breaking News! Breaking News! Breaking News! Breaking News! Breaking News!
A new study shows that life has side-effects. While life was developed as a benefit to society and as a general panacea, one group has been leading the internet charge against it, claiming that it has far worse side-effects than the benefits it bestows. The titular leader of the group released a statement yesterday, "There are things they don't want you to know about life. We're here to reveal the truth! Life has been shown to cause pain, diarrhea, vomiting, seizures, weight loss, weight gain, genetic abnormalities, cancer, and even death. That's right! Life causes death. Without life, there wouldn't be any death! And that's what they're keeping from you!" This group is looking to stop the production of life. As of this writing, the creator of life has not released a response to these accusations. Those against life see this lack of defense as a justification to continue their endeavors. "Because they have no defense! Which just proves they know all the bad stuff that life does to people and animals and yet continue to callously produce it!" Once they get life eliminated this group's plan is to go after water and oxygen as both of these can cause harm in sufficient quantities, leading to water intoxication and oxidative damage of lung tissue. "Water is the leading cause of drowning!" they contend.

"Well, I'll do some research on your recommended Product X before I decide."

"Yes, you do that. Go do your "research" that <u>no one</u> else has ever done before you."

*****

"I want pain medication that eliminates all pain, has no side-effects, and doesn't cause sedation."

Oh, no, no, no. I don't use any flea products on him. I don't believe in using all those chemicals on my pets.

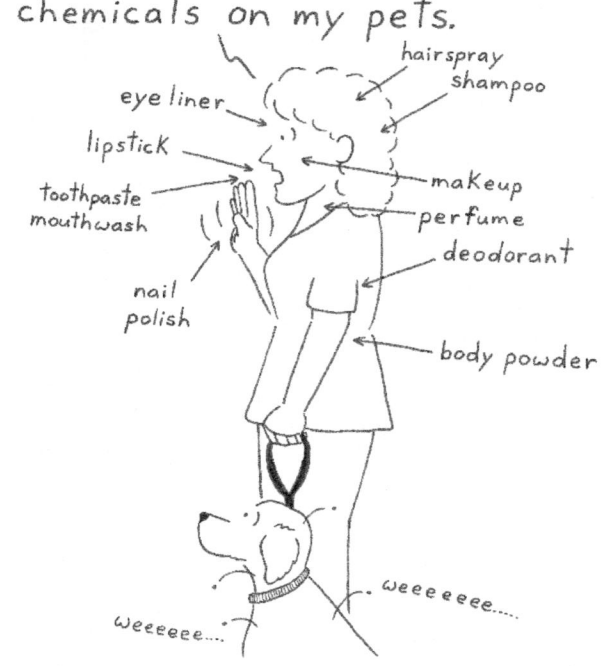

*****

Oh, sure, we can do that. If you want me to practice 19th century medicine!

The Veterinary Technician Everyone Knows

How is it that everyone knows a veterinary technician? You know what I mean. They're the vet tech that "lives next door" or "used to work at their previous clinic" or "my sister knows" or "a friend who lives somewhere else now". And this mystery person is always brought up to justify some strange thing that the client has done. "I put yogurt in the ears because he has an ear infection." "I put cornstarch in the pee-pee folds to fight off yeast." "I've been adding colloidal silver to the water to help heal her broken leg." All advice placed firmly at the feet of the authority of the unknown vet tech.

I think they're an urban legend. You know, like the Vet Tech With The Hook For A Hand or The Hitchhiking Vet Tech. Outside of my clinic, I don't know anyone who is a vet tech. Yet, a great portion of my clients seem to know someone who is or has been one. But if you try to pin them down, suddenly it's two- or three-people removed from them, like some veterinary version of Six Degrees From Kevin Bacon. And no one can ever produce an actual person or phone number where you can contact the mystery tech and tell them to stop dispensing bad advice. Sometimes I think there must be only one person (maybe it IS Kevin Bacon), because the same bad advice crops up from different clients. Either one person is just very busy undermining the profession or vet techs are as common as sneezes in cold season; maybe they're as common as the clients who all claim they're "nurses". On-line, everyone seems to be a vet tech. But, then, everyone on-line is beautiful, intelligent, and wealthy also. I do appreciate the ones on-line who identify that they are not a veterinarian or a veterinary technician and then go on to give wrong advice anyway. And the fact that people will just accept information no matter how outlandish is appalling too. I'm certain the reason for this is because the perception is that the person giving the advice has no financial motivation. This is wrongly seen as good advice because it is free, with no one remembering the adage, "You get what you pay for."

Wonder if I could get away with it. "Yeah, well, I'm not an auto mechanic, but I think if you just jigger this little valve here in the anacanafranastan, you shouldn't have to take it in. Now, if it explodes on you, then you probably didn't do it like I said." I think the urban vet tech legend is our profession's more specific answer to "They". As in, "you know what *they* say" or "*they* say (fill in inane comment here)". It's that ambiguous, ephemeral nonsense that we fight every day and yet it has the tenacity of a starved pit-bull in the minds of the public. I'm constantly amazed, here in the 21st Century, knowing how much good information we dispense daily, that we still have to battle against what can only be termed a Force of Nature; one called Ignorance. And, unlike hurricanes, there is no season for it.

Human-Animal Bond

The phrase "Human-Animal Bond" has been around throughout my schooling and career. It's a rah-rah catch-phrase that's supposed to rally the wagons into a circle of mutual understanding and compassion. Yet, as the years have passed, I have started to think that the phrase, like Inigo Montoya observed, does not mean what we think it means. The AVMA defines it this way: "The human-animal bond is a mutually beneficial and dynamic relationship between people and animals that is influenced by behaviors that are essential to the health and well-being of both." We are promoters of the human-animal bond. We make assumptions that our clients are part of the human-animal bond and we're supposed to celebrate pet ownership with this in mind. Don't get me wrong here, I know for a fact that people benefit enormously from animals. I believe in the human-animal bond. Yet I think we're like missionaries preaching ineffectually to a subset of people who don't share the same language. I do not think the human-animal bond is as ubiquitous as we think it is or operates in a manner by which we would like.

What started me thinking about this was when I ran across a couple of mentions in different venues that we, the veterinary profession, prey upon the human-animal bond and exploit it to our own nefarious ends (financial, of course). Certainly, the sources for these types of accusations are suspect. Leave it to people to find the worst way to depict what is otherwise a positive force and use it in an insulting way. I'm sure if you pinned down these people they would not be able to adequately defend their position, but in a way their opinion didn't really include me anyway. Because I don't really think about the human-animal bond; it is not a part of my every day internal dialogue. Therefore, I really don't know how I'd go about exploiting it.

I'm aware of it, of course, and I admit, it's nice when you see it, when you experience it yourself. There are certainly people who have that deep emotional attachment to their animals. It seems to be a small percentage of the population that I see, though. When we all believe in something, we tend to hang around with people who agree with us. That is a good and natural thing when it comes to the human-animal bond amongst those in the veterinary profession. However, the general population doesn't seem to be as influenced by this outlook as we are. For example, in the AVMA definition it is said to be to the "health and well-being of both (people and animals)." I don't see animals benefiting as much from this bond as people do. I have a fair percentage of people who will only bring a pet to the veterinarian if they have a problem and, often, it has to be a pretty big problem for them to do this. And frequently it has to be a problem that affects the owner. A torn cruciate does not necessarily motivate an owner to fix it. Urinating on new furniture, however? That will probably get a pet brought in. Then there are those we've seen that aren't motivated to treat even the big problems. In the mean-time these pets are really getting only the minimum definition of care: food, shelter, water. I wonder why some people have pets. I've had people who have only done three-year rabies vaccines (a step up from nothing), just bawl when putting their heartworm positive dog down. Through tears they have told me, "He was the best dog ever!" And at seven years of age was the oldest dog they'd ever had. Now, there's certainly some human-animal bond working here, but not to the benefit of the pet. I had one client I've mentioned before, who had a wonderful, bright and perky eight-year old Lab with a mass that was huge but just this side of operable that I recommended such. He sat back in his chair and said, "Well, Doc, let's be honest. He's just not worth it." And here was this dog obviously completely devoted, looking up with love and wagging his tail at this callous man. I thought to myself, "The only reason you feel it's ok to say that is because your dog doesn't understand your words." While he is a stand-out in my mind, I, and you I suspect, have a long list of similar encounters with owner. It starts to make you wonder if this human-animal bond thing is akin to Sasquatch or the Loch Ness Monster.

And then there is the flip-side to the equation and that is where the human-animal bond gets used against us. This almost invariably revolves around money or doing something more for someone. This is when certain animal-related groups come to us and want services and our time and it should be given freely and willingly because, you know, the human-animal bond. Even if you participate, you need to set a limit because these groups will often want more than you're willing or able to do. To say 'no' to something is to not care enough and casts you in a dim light in their eyes. The phrase "you don't care" that a client can whip out faster than Liberty Valance with a gun is just a slap at our belief system regarding the human-animal bond. Except it isn't. It's a tactic. It's actually a reflection of their lack of a bond with the animal, expecting others to take up the slack in that bond, financially and emotionally.

Why do I bring this type of ugliness up? Because it needs to be acknowledged. Sometimes we are the only advocates for animals. I like to say that I'm not doing this job for the client, I'm doing this job for the pet. Hopefully the client gets some benefit from doing my job. Our belief in a human-animal bond is much stronger than many of the people we meet through our practices. And it's hard to be the one who cares more about the pet than the owner does. This is where "compassion fatigue" resides. While you will, you cannot care more than the owner. You will take that home with you day after day and it will eat you up. We all have to find some way to run this emotional gauntlet. We have to set limits as to what we are able to handle, how much we are willing to put ourselves out there. And this has to happen if we expect to have long, productive careers. "First Do No Harm" applies to us personally as well.

General Thoughts

I hope this next section doesn't come across as trite. These are just some additional thoughts I have had that I think help realign our perspective. You'll find a lot of my approach is self-protective. Again, some of this advice may not work for you and that's okay. I just figure if these things have helped me, I'm sure others will find them useful.

When criticism rains down on us in the veterinary field like ash from Mt. St. Helen's, it's important to remind ourselves that we are *good people.* And that we have surrounded ourselves with good people, and we tell our staff we know they are good people. This is important because there are times clients will insist we aren't good people. While I'll defend myself, I don't feel the need to convince these clients I'm a good person. I already know that. A lot of things get unfairly laid in our laps, and good luck trying to get clients, who aren't otherwise inclined, to see us as well-intentioned. Yes, they're going to go off and spew their unfavorable viewpoint here, there and yonder. So what? I know I'm a good person and I know my staff are good people and that is all that matters at the end of the day. It helps to have trust in your employees as well so clients can't use things against them or you. I've laughed when a client has told me something absurd that supposedly had been said by a one of my staff or my office manager. I knew them well enough that there was no way they would have said such a thing. Conversely, my staff knows me well enough that they know when a client is trying to manipulate them by invoking my name to facilitate something and yet it doesn't sound like something I'd say.

No matter how bad a day is, it will end. On one particular bad day, I kept telling my staff, "Hey, look, no matter what, we are going to be done at 5 o'clock. Five. The magic number is *fiiiiiiiive*." It's easy to get caught up in the tidal wave of angst after dealing with a clenched-sphincter of a human being. I think sometimes that's what they want and that's why they behave the way they do. They're trying to provoke a confrontation. However, if we let it to continue to affect us, they have won. And, while I'm not 100 percent good at this, I will tell you that it is a relief to take a breath and remind myself that these kinds of days are finite. One of my technicians seemed tired upon entering work, so I asked her how she was. She said it just seems like the day is going to be so long. I told her when I feel this way (every day) I break it down. I look at, "It's four hours until lunch" and then after lunch, "It's four hours until we close." I've even gone so far as to countdown how many patients I still have to see and if one client is bringing in two patients, I only count them as one! Maybe it's a terrible admission, but this inchworm effect is how I often get through a shift. Or a year.

An example away from practice may help. I was at a Wendy's. I had ordered and stepped aside, waiting for my food. I overhear the next customer ask for a burger and he wanted it to have tomato. Then he started objecting to the cashier because it rang up as an "add-on". He insisted it's not an "add-on", that the definition of a burger includes tomato. At this point I was thinking, *oh, look, a client.* The flustered cashier tried to assure him that there isn't an additional charge (as if that were the problem) and that if he wanted a tomato on his burger, she had to put the line item in adding it. He's incensed. He says, "I've had this problem before!" Which I thought was particularly revealing. If you've had this problem before, then it's been addressed, but for some reason, perhaps attention, you wish to continue to come here and be mortally offended. That's on you, dude. He went on, pointing, "Look at all of these pictures of burgers! They all have tomato on them!" Now, at this point, I was so glad I wasn't the cashier, because I would've said, "Yes, sir, that's true. And those were all 'add-ons'." I got my food and did not hear how all this resolved. I'm sure the people in line behind this guy were thrilled with the delay. I'm sure the cashier will have an indelible memory of this encounter, as well. I so wanted to lean in and tell him, "You know what? There are people starving in Haiti. They literally have no food! They would kill for a burger without tomato. Perhaps you should take your displaced anger issues somewhere else." I didn't do this, in case you were wondering, because I've found that I tend to make situations worse rather than better. Remember "Tomato Guy" when you're dealing with an enraged client. How much of what they're purporting they're upset about is valid and how much is about condiments.

In preparation for vet school, we took animal science courses, zoology, biology, etc. We took the prerequisites as well as ones we thought would ensure us a shot at vet school. What we weren't told is that these would be virtually useless in a practice setting. Instead we should emphasize psychiatric or social sciences. Because I find that I need more help in those areas trying to navigate the murky psychology of clients. I know it seems like I pick on clients a lot, but I'm really only talking about the behaviors and situations they present that make our jobs more difficult and therefore hinder our ability to help their animals. We talk a lot about changing our protocols and our own behaviors as a reaction to clients without acknowledging that there are some things that we just cannot control or finesse. We seem to always be finding fault with ourselves when what needs to be addressed is the abusive or recalcitrant client. Don't get me wrong. I am fully aware that there are many stable people out there. We need to change the paradigm of "oh, how can I make this angry person happy?" to "how much of this am I going to tolerate?".

I have what I call the "six-month rule". If you start looking, you'll find it's applicable in your practice as well. After assessing a client complaint, you may often find it to be based on pet peeve, whim, entitlement, or misperception. If you have a client who has gone to 12 on the anger scale for something that's really more on the level of "I said I wanted mayo on the side!", look at the chart and see how long they've been coming to your practice. If it is less than six months, I guarantee you these people go to 12 over the tiniest of perceived slights done to them everywhere they go. They've been rewarded in the past for such behavior. They have learned to yell in order to get their way. They've been yelling at others since they came out of the womb. Do not try too hard to appease these people. You can't. Even if you do in the short-term, you've set yourself up for an on-going abusive relationship. Just as a pet may learn to object to a certain level of handling in order to not have their nails trimmed, so too have clients learned. And we know not to automatically give in to a struggling pet because when the next nail trim comes around, they will ratchet up their objection. As will a client.

One, perhaps morbid positive I find with the over-reactors is they at least make it very clear, right up front, they're going to be an on-going problem. It makes it a bit easier for me to dismiss their insults and crabbing and not internalize them. And often I get the benefit of a cartoon idea.

We put up with a lot of bad behavior from clients. A lot. I know some of you are nodding out there and can readily think of a few clients who try everyone's patience when they visit. I think our entire profession puts up with more than we should. I think we get inured and have a pretty high tolerance for people's behavior. We have to set boundaries, however, of what we consider acceptable.

Understand, I'm talking about situation where you might feel bewildered as to why a client is angry and their behavioral display makes you doubt yourself. That's actually the reason for their behavioral display. This is where the six-month rule comes in handy. It clarifies things. They've been a client for less than six months? Be suspicious as to their motivations and emotional veracity.

Ever been given the ultimatum, "I'm never coming back here!"? This is a negotiation step, not an actual plan of action. You can tell this because they don't actually leave then, they pause. They're awaiting the next step in the bartering ritual. The implication is you have one last chance to bend to their demand and they'll stay. My answer? "Go ahead. You're an adult. You have choices in life. Go find somewhere else to be happy. And may God help the next practice you go to." Or something to that effect. I don't like being yelled at and I've been yelled at a lot for so many minor quibbles and clients' idiosyncracies. I fully understand helping or apologizing to a client for something legitimate. And I have. They get a different response from me. Those situations are very rare. We get way more of the trifling complaint that people then want to inflate. It takes a toll on us. I hope the six-month rule takes some of the personal burden off of you; these situations have more to do with the internal illogic and scattered emotionality of the client and nothing to do with you. Their abuse is just another tactic in their arsenal. They insult. They guilt. They're bullies. Recognize them as such and don't let them push you around or make you feel bad about yourself.

Our job is difficult, and I recognize that. And while it is work, I strive to have as much fun as possible, for both myself and my staff, in a work setting. That doesn't mean we cut-up all the time or can't be serious. But I think we need to take moments and recognize the absurdities that arise in life and find humor in them. For me, regardless of how bad a day may be, I can usually find some way to make it into a cartoon, share it with others and, hopefully, give them something to recognize, chuckle at and realize that we're all dealing with the same things.

One of the ways we can help each other is in sharing our experiences. I believe in school, as well as practice, we feel isolated; just look at the number of single doctor practices. When an owner is yelling at us in an unseemly fashion, our inclination is to think we've done something wrong. Very often that's not the case. Some people are yellers. They yell at the grocery store cashier, they yell at their mechanic, they yell at their spouse, they yell at you. It's how they approach life. It's easy to take personally when it happens. However, I've found when I share my stories, particularly of client encounters, other vets and staff recognize they've been in similar situations. It's a relief to them to realize that it's not them, it's the client. It's revealing to other vets to see that this is what people do and it's not personal, which somehow makes my thoughts about humanity worse if you think about human behavior in general; that they yell and fuss and demand and demean to get what they want without regard of who they hurt. More often than not, the yelling stems from something in them, not anything that you've done. You're just the convenient target at that time. Doesn't make it right. Also, doesn't mean you have to attend to their particular lunacy or allow yourself to be the casualty of their blunt weapon brand of criticism.

"That? Oh, that's my veterinary degree. But, I found I could make a better living selling pot."

*****

Having to get through the owner's defensive line to treat their pet

SELF-INTEREST APATHY EXCUSES FINANCES

170

"I know we said that you should marry a doctor, but we didn't mean a veterinarian."

*****

He sometimes eats chocolate after a particularly difficult client.

My God! Who did he see?!

Well, you know, you have to understand.... she was abused.

That's what they say about every vet!

*****

I guess I don't need to ask who's dominant in this relationship.

"You remember that lady from yesterday?"

"The one with the dog in the morning."

"The one with the endless questions?"

"You know, the crazy one!"

"Still not narrowing it down."

*****

"I'll see your vet "experience" and raise you "I've had German Shepherds since I was a kid"."

Veterinary medicine as card game

No, I'm here on my own. Let's face it, if I had to wait for my owner to bring me, I'd never get here.

*****

blah blah blah blah blahbitty blah blah blah blahzy blah blah blah blah blah blah blahblahblahblahblahblahzinnyblahblahblah blahbitty blahzitty blah blah blah blahzy blah blah blah blahblahblahblahblah blahbitty blahzinny blah blah blahzy blahblahblah blah blah blah blah blah hahahahahaha blah blah blah blahbitty blah blah blahnzy blah blah blah blahbitty blah blah blahz blah blahblahblah blahbitty blah blahbinny blah blah blah blahblahblah blahz blahzy blahzzy blah blah blah blah blah lahlahlahla blah blizzy blizzy blah blah blah blahbitty blah blah ah hahahaha blahzinny blah blah bl ah bla h blahzinny blahzy blah blahblah bl ahblabbity blahblahbl ah bl a h blahzy blah blahbity b la h bla h blahblah blah blah bl ah bl ahblahblah

Do you ever feel yourself physically aging in the room?

At the veterinarian's party there were separate entrances for cat and dog people

hiss! hiss!

Grrrrrr....

*****

— I don't accept that answer! I want you to ask the doctor!

— Seen any good movies lately?
— No, not really, but there's some pretty good stuff on Petflix.
— I'm going to see that new Marvel movie!
— Oh yeah! Can't wait!

— There's a new app where you can see a movie a day for only $10!
— Wow! Really? That seems too good to be true.
— I'm going to give it a try! Let me know if it works!
— Sure!

He said 'no'.

"Oh, my god! He's huge! He....he's enormous! Everyone! Come look how fat this dog is!"

Sometimes, don't you just want to?

*****

"I'm never coming back here!"

"Yeah? Me neither! This place sucks!"

"My daughter wants to be a vet!"

Eight years old. Unspayed. Never on heartworm prevention. Last vaccines: a 3-year rabies done 5 years ago

*****

Dr. Smith shows submissive behavior to the senior veterinarian.

I've been coming here for 'X' amount of years and spent 'Y' amount of money and...gripe, complain, accuse, insult....!!

Deflectors! Full Intensity!

whew.

*****

Have you heard about (insert latest crazy fad here)? I found it on malecattlefeces.com.

The Light Stuff

Sequential Cartoons

This next section is a combination of words and cartoons to convey certain concepts. It acts as a pretty good approximation as to how my brain works on a normal day.

There is a group of people that use the veterinarian as their town hall, counselor, social worker, psychiatrist, secondary personal physician, etc. A visit to pick up a tube of flea prevention can occupy a good couple of hours. A sub-set of this group are the Just-Five-Minutes People. They're called this because they just need five minutes of your time to digest six years of history from a previous veterinarian to see if it's worthwhile for them to bring their pet in to actually see you. They can also be current clients who just need the doctor's ear for "five minutes" to plead their case and describe imprecise and amorphous symptoms that they hope to parlay into "just getting some medication" without having to bring in their pet. We become the Fortune Cookie Doctor – the tiny, rectangular piece of paper reads: "The tumor will be benign." You can string enough "five minutes" in a row on a typical day and find you haven't accomplished anything, except perhaps to annoy some people with answers they don't wish to hear. There are times I watch the time on the telephone pass and feel like hanging up right at the five-minute mark. Spoiler alert, it's never five minutes.

Then there are the One-More-Thing People. These are the people who seem to not want to be parted from you, who can't quit you. You've been in the room and addressed in detail what they were in for originally, you go to leave, and suddenly they say, "Oh, wait. One more thing." Then you address that. Try to leave. "One more thing." And it just seems to go on and on. As if touching the doorknob is their behavioral queue to ask another question. I've even asked, after a few rounds of this type of Jeopardy, "Anything else? Any other problems? No? That's it? Ok." Touch the doorknob and what do you know – "Wait! One more thing!"

Unlike lawyers, however, we do not charge by the hour. Therefore, here are some options you can use:

   For the Five-Minute-People:
   1) hide in the back (you've probably already tried this one)
   OR.......
   2) staff runs interference (again probably used regularly)

For the Talkers and the One-More-Thing People:
1) fake your own death (unfortunately, even this may not always work)

"Oh, that reminds me of a Boxer I had who died suddenly...."

OR.......

2) get animatronic replica of yourself

"So, I said, 'Hey, that's my weedwhacker!' Then, he said,...."

"How... interesting.. ...I...must...write ..that....down."

OR…….

3) attempt distraction

"Look! James Herriot!"

OR…….

4) use the taxicab system for visits where you put the meter flag up as you're going into the room and the owner can see how much it is costing them over time. This will have one of two effects:

   a) it will make them get to the point without detours regarding their cousin's dog in another state or their thoughts on the beneficial aspects of snail livers

   OR…….

   b) they'll just continue to talk as always, but at least you'll be getting properly compensated for your time

OR…….

5) hire them (if they're going to be around so long anyway, they may as well help out)

You would think that vet school would have aged us enough physically that we wouldn't get grief about looking "too young to be the vet". Now, this has never happened to me personally, but I've heard from others. And it's ironic that a youthful appearance, which is usually a complimentary reference, in our profession is considered a detriment. I find it distinctly amusing to hear this observation from people who are only in for nail trims. In truth, new graduates are probably at the peak of their game. By the time you get to my age, you've forgotten more than you remember. Granted, it's a bit like whittling away the extraneous, less useful material until you arrive at the underlying sculpture, but we don't give enough credit to new grads for bringing fresh insight and contemporary thinking to a practice. Even babies look at the world with fresh eyes and an innocent wisdom that we, as adults, have outgrown.

Youth implies a lack of experience, which of course may not necessarily be true. Good judgment comes from experience; experience comes from bad judgment. If there's a quota system for mistakes, you could have made all of yours already and are now on the upswing to doing everything right!

It's interesting, also, that we don't want people to do the opposite and say, "Wow, you are really old. Like carbon-dating old! Here, let me help you. That syringe looks heavy."

Should a client make reference to you looking "too young", you can either calmly and maturely thank them and state that you are, indeed, the veterinarian and move on, or you can do the following:

1) leave and send in the teenage kennel person to give the client perspective

OR.......

2) act stupid

I also find it amusing that when we do get to be an older vet, now we're viewed by some as "old school" and not up-to-date on things. I think there's like a 20-minute window between where people don't consider us too young and inexperienced ***and*** don't consider us too old and set-in-our-ways. I'm not sure at what point that window passes, but I have a feeling I was in the bathroom at the time and missed it.

One of my favorite situations is when the client who knows least about the pet is the one who brings them in. You know you're in trouble when a spouse, roommate, distant relative, Facebook friend, pulls out a crumpled piece of paper that contains either a list of questions or symptoms or both. Conversations usually proceed like this:

Another interesting area is the comments we hear over and over again:

"We wormed him with something over-the-counter, so we know that's not the problem."
Interpretation: pet has rounds, hooks, whips, giardia, coccidia, and tapeworms

"He's got ear mites, but they don't go away with the stuff from the feed store."
Interpretation: bilateral ear infection

"Oh, no, she's strictly an indoor cat."
Interpretation: the little hussy's out at all hours

"I've never seen fleas on him."
Interpretation: flea allergy dermatitis

There are a couple of ways you can deal with these comments:

1) wear a gun

OR……if there's a waiting period in your state and you need immediate action

2) use negative reinforcement techniques

Sometimes, communication with clients is all too clear:

Let's talk next about fractious, touchy, irritable, cross, unmanageable, or otherwise, peevish pets.

It's like some kind of test of our reflexes. You almost get the impression the client has a stopwatch to measure your response time. "Oooooo…..I'm sorry, we're going to have to see another veterinarian. You were much too slow." Or possibly, "Hey, nice! You were a lot faster than the last vet we saw!"

And there's always a reason for the pet reacting adversely. Stop me if you've heard any (or all) of the following (of course, you really can't stop me, because this has already been written, so maybe I should say, stop reading if you've heard any of the following):

"He was abused before we got him."

"You handled him too roughly."

"She's a rescue."

"You must have startled him."

"He's only like this at the vet's."

"He's been like this ever since...(fill in the blank)
1) "they were boarded"   2) "they were groomed"
3) "they were spayed/neutered"
4) "the last vet's office I went to"
but never fill in the blank with "they were born"

"He's not a morning dog."

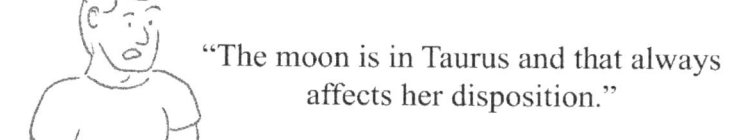

"The moon is in Taurus and that always affects her disposition."

Then you sometimes get that extra bit of information that you just really didn't need to hear (while you're bandaging the lacerations on your hand): "He's never been like this with other veterinarians." Later on, should they be at a different clinic, some clients get to use the excuse that their pet wasn't like this before they took them to see you. This last excuse can pretty much be used throughout the lifetime of the animal.

I often want to respond with, "It could just be that your 'pet' is an unruly, aggressive malcontent with antisocial tendencies."

Just once, I'd like to hear a little bit of honesty from the client, such as in the next cartoon:

Other DVMs You Might Know

"Why do you come here if you're not going to listen any way?!! AAAAAAAAAAAAA"

Sam Kinison, DVM

*****

"Help me help you!"

Jerry Maguire, DVM

I'm getting too old for this shit.
Roger Murtaugh, DVM

*****

OK! OK! I'll take better care of him!
Yes!
Ronda Rousey, DVM

"Yeah, well, you know, that's just like your opinion, man."

The Dude, DVM

*****

I don't ▓▓▓ remember telling you to open up your stupid mouth! I dare you! I double-dare you, ▓▓▓-▓▓▓, to open up your dumb pie-hole one more time! Do you have a veterinary degree hidden up your ▓▓▓?! I didn't think so! Now, sit down, take notes, and I'll ▓▓▓ TELL you how to take care of your ▓▓▓-▓▓▓ prissy ▓▓▓!

Samuel L. Jackson, DVM

199

Once you see the patients still waiting in exam rooms 1, 2, and 3, stabilize the HBC, unblock the cat, get x-rays on that Dane, do your call-backs, discharge your in-patients, and make sure the surgeries are recovering, THEN you can go to the Ball.

Just remember - you're on-call.

Dr. Cinderella - associate veterinarian

*****

We've made too many compromises already; too many retreats. They invade our space and we fall back. They make even more unreasonable demands and we fall back. Not again. The line must be drawn here! This far! No further! And I will make them pay for what they've done!

Jean-Luc Picard, DVM has one bad client encounter too many

The Vet With The Pet
(with apologies to the other Dr.)

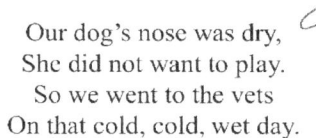

Our dog's nose was dry,
She did not want to play.
So we went to the vets
On that cold, cold, wet day.

I went there with Sally.
We went there, we two.
And I said, "How I wish
We hadn't forgotten the poo!"

The vet was behind,
The phone rang off the wall.
So we sat in the clinic.
We did nothing at all.

So all we could do was to
Sit! Sit! Sit! Sit!
And we did not like it,
Not one little bit.

And then,
Something went BUMP!
How that bump made us jump!

We looked!
Then we saw him, his pant leg all wet!
We looked!
And we saw him!
The vet for our pet!
And he said to us,
"I do believe you are next!"

"I'm glad you are here
And sorry your dog, Flower, is in the dumps.
But we can
Prod, poke, and squeeze her 'til she eats and she jumps!"

"I know some good tests we could run."
Said the vet.
"I know some new tricks."
Said the vet to our pet.
"A lot of good tricks.
I will show them to you.
I hope you
Will not mind at all if I do."

Then Sally and I
Did not know what to say.
It was apparent our vet was out of his mind
For the day.

But our dog (to our surprise) said, "No! No!
Make that vet go away!
Tell that vet with the debt
You do not want to pay.
I'm feeling better now.
Watch me frisk about.
Don't let him touch me
While his mind is still out!"

"Now! Now! Have no fear.
Have no fear!" said the vet.
"My tests are not bad."
Said the vet to our pet.
"Why, we can have
Lots of good fun, if you try,
With a game that I call
'Watch the Fur Fly'!"

"Stop chasing me about," said our dog.
"This is no fun at all!
Stop chasing me about," said our dog.
"Think you're so tough 'cause you're tall!"

"Have no fear!" said the vet.
"I will not let you jump.
I will hold you <u>real</u> tight.
So, your little head won't 'bump'.
With a syringe in one hand!
And a muzzle to get!
I need but a few more things!"
Said the vet.....

"Look at me!
Look at me now!" said the vet.
"With syringe and muzzle
And a well-placed elbow set!
I can hold him down
Until the count of ten!
I can hold him down
Until he says, "When!"
Oh, crap!
He hops up and down like a ball!
But, that is not all!
Oh, no.
That is not all.....

"Look at me!
Look at me!
Look at me now!
Don't try this at home
You have to know how.
The muzzle is off
But his blood I did take!
Then again, it could be
My blood, for Heaven's sake!"

"What cute little teeth.
A good cleaning's what they need!
But, first let's pause,
To find where from I bleed!
Oh, look! My shirt's torn.
Don't you look so smug!
You and your pink bow!
You're just a smug walking rug!
And, oh, no.
That is not all....."

That is what the vet said.....
Then he fell on his head!
He went down with a thud
His face drained of color.
And Sally and I
Were quite proud of our Flower!

And our dog came down, too.
She jumped onto the floor!
The vet began to sit up.
Our dog went to the door.
"I must put my paw down.
This once! This is it!
No, I do not like it,
Not one little bit!"
"Now look what you did!"
Said our pet to the vet.
"Now, look at this room!
Look at me! Don't forget!
You mussed my new 'do.
My bow is akilter.
I chipped a tooth on your watch
And you've never looked guiltier.
You should not be here
When your mind is not.
I am leaving this clinic!"
Said our pet who was hot!

"But, I like to be here.
Oh, I like it a lot!"
Said the vet to our pet
And then added, "Not!"
"Do not go away.
You are sick. You can't go!
And so," said the vet to our pet,
"So, so, so.....
I will show you
Another good game that I know!"

And then he ran out.
And then, fast as a fox,
The vet with the debt,
Came back in with a box.

A big red wood box.
It was shut with a hook.
"Now look at my help."
Said the vet.
"Take a look!"

Then he got up on top
With a pant leg still wet.
"I call this game Help-In-A-Box,"
Said the vet.

"In this box are two people.
I will show them to you now.
You will like these two people,"
Said the vet with a bow.

"I will pick up this hook.
You will see something new.
Two people. And I call them
Tech One and Tech Two.
These techs will not bite you.
They want to have fun."
Then, out of the box
Came Tech Two and Tech One!
And they ran to us fast.
They said, "How do you do?"
"Would you like to shake hands
With Tech One and Tech Two?"

And Sally and I
Did not know what to do.
So we had to shake hands
With Tech One and Tech Two.
We shook their hands
But our dog said, "Not them!
Do not shake their hands!
You don't know where they've been!
They should not be here!
Overpower me they will not!
Let me out! Let me out!"
Said our pet who was still hot!

"Have no fear, little Flower,"
Said the vet to our pet.
"These Techs are good Techs,"
And he reached for a net.
"They are so tame. Oh, so tame!
They have come here to play.
They will give you some x-rays.
How about that? What do you say?"

"Now, here is a game that they like,"
Said the vet.
"They call it a Half-Nelson,"
Said the vet to our pet.

"No! Not in the back room!"
Said our pet who was caught.
"They should not take me
To the back room! They should not!
Oh, the things they will do to me!
How I'll fuss, squirm, and squeal!
Oh, I do not like it!
Let's make a deal!"

Then Sally and I
Saw them run down the hall.
We saw those two Techs
Bang their heads on the wall!
Bump! Thump! Thump! Bump!
On the wall in the hall.

Tech Two and Tech One!
They ran up! They ran down!
One got the gloves.
The other the gowns!
Flower let loose words
That turned our ears red.
As the techs straddled the table
And sat on her head!

Then those Techs ran about
With big bumps, jumps, and kicks.
It seemed the machine had a short,
And that was some trick!
And I said,
"I do not like the way that they play!
If a lawyer could see this,
Oh, what would they say?"

Then our dog said, "Look! Look!"
Sparks jumped from our doggie dear.
"Let's talk about this calmly.
OK? Do you hear?"
The vet slowly approached
And said, "How do you feel?"
Our pet said, "Zzzzzzz.....zzzzzzz.....
I think I need to be healed."

"So, do something! Fast!" said our dog.
"Do you hear?
I see a bright light!
The end is coming near!"
The vet said, "As fast as I can
I must think of something to do!
I will have to get help from
Tech One and Tech Two!"

The Techs were still bouncing
Around like two jets.
The vet said, "With my net
I can get them I bet.
I bet with my net,
I can get those Techs yet!"

Then he let down his net.
It came down with a PLOP!
And he had them! At last!
Those two Techs had been stopped.
Then I said to the vet,
"Now you do what I say.
You and these Techs
Help our dog! Find a way!"

"Oh, dear!" said the vet.
"You are looking to blame.....
Oh, dear.
What a shame!
What a shame!
What a shame!

Then he and the Techs
Got equipment and books.
And they went into surgery
To give Flower a look.

"This is not good," said the Techs.
"But we can fix her. Yes.
Get the anesthesia
And we will fix this big mess!
But this mess is so big
And so deep and so tall.
It will take hours to sew up.
Can we fix it at all?"

And then!
Who was back in his mind?
Why, the vet!
"Have no fear of this mess,"
Said the vet to the Techs.
"I always pick up my messes
And so.....
I will show you another
Good trick that I know!"

Then we saw him pick out
Our pet's brain from her head.
"She does not use this anyway,"
Or so our vet said.
"Only one kidney is needed
And two lungs is redundant too.
This intestine's too long
And her gums look good blue.
Most dogs do fine with only three legs."
And he gave little Flower a pat.
Then he was done.
And he said, "That is that."

Then we went home.
We went home, we two.
And we put our pet in her bed
Like we normally do.

And Sally and I did not know
What to say.
So we patted
Her empty head and called it a day.

Whatever the vet did
Flower is doing well.
She drools and she stares
But, she doesn't bark at the doorbell.
She's stopped that constant yipping
And does not trip us crossing the floor.
If we'd known how good she'd be
We would have paid more.

Clientese

Our veterinary advice magazines love nothing better than putting the entire onus on our shoulders for proper communication, ignoring the fact that there is another person involved in any conversation. Or people if we include the spouse, aunt, sister, grandmother, child, etc. as well who niggle their way in. The articles insist that as long as we spend hours with a client, repeating things over and over again, using common words so as not to threaten or demean a person's fragile psychology, and speak in a soft, NPR voice of mutual care and respect, we will be able to get them to understand and comply with our recommendations. If you've gotten this far in the book, you probably know what direction I'll be coming from. Even when speaking the same language, communication is specious at best.

What follows are examples I've accumulated over the years translating Clientese (this is a local dialect variation of indigenous language seen in every culture). Some common aspects of this you probably already know. For example, doubling the time a client tells you that a problem has been going on. "Two days" is actually "two weeks", etc. Police officers are aware of this phenomenon when they're told the person has only had "a couple of beers" after being pulled over. And most of you know to halve the amount a client tells you they spent at a previous veterinary practice. A completely different translational approach is taken when negotiating the estimate down with you, where *the client* will halve the price of what they spent elsewhere to somehow shame or guilt you into matching these previous fictional rates. Knowing which dialect a client is speaking is important in distinguishing these modes of "communication". What follows are examples of what a client says translated to what they really mean.

1. Client describes their dog as "shy" or "skittish" or "they're just talking"
   Interpretation: "He'll kill you. Kill you dead."
2. "He got into my sister's brownies."
   Interpretation: "He ate my whole stash."
3. "Dr. X (the vet) is a good friend of mine."
   Interpretation: "Dr. X has no idea who I am."
   (as a side note, I've told my staff that if a client ever tries to use this ploy, they are free and clear to tell them, "Dr. Docsway doesn't have any friends.")
4. When their pet is "late on vaccines"
   Interpretation: "not vaccinated"
5. "I don't have paperwork (vaccines, bloodwork, receipts, etc.)"
   Interpretation: "Paperwork doesn't exist in this reality."
6. "indoor cat" = "indoor cat"
   "strictly indoor cat" = "outdoor cat"
   "outdoor cat" = "I'm not putting money into this cat"
   "neighborhood cat" = "not my cat" + "outdoor cat"

7. "I only give a tiny, itsy-bitsy, molecule piece of people food on a rare occasion."
   Interpretation: "He eats what I eat."
8. "We don't feed people food."
   Interpretation: "We don't feed people food that you'll find out about."
9. On phone (late to their appointment): "I'm only five minutes away."
   Interpretation: "I'm five minutes away from being a half-hour away."
10. "They've had all their shots."
    Interpretation: "They haven't had any shots." (usually combined with #5 above)
11. "My spouse takes care of that (bathing, heartworm meds, etc.)"
    Interpretation: "No one takes care of that."
12. "I'll need to talk to my spouse about it."
    Interpretation: "We're not going to do what you're asking."
13. "Can I get an estimate?"
    Interpretation: "I need to look like I've earnestly considered something before rejecting it."
14. "We don't have any money."
    Interpretation: "What can you do for us?" and/or "We have money, but not for that."
15. "I don't remember the name of the flea medication I use, but I use it every month."
    Interpretation: "I don't use any flea control."
16. "He's vomiting."
    Interpretation: "He vomited once, two weeks ago."
17. "He's not eating."
    Interpretation: "not eating as much" or "not eating people food" or "not eating like I think he should" or "not eating dog food, but eats people food and treats just fine"
18. "He's never bit anyone."
    Interpretation: "….because he's always muzzled first." or "He's never connected with a bite because the other people were fast."
19. "Ate a toy, stick, etc."
    Interpretation: "chewed up" a toy, stick, etc., not actually "ate" or "ingested"
20. "rescued"
    Interpretation: "adopted" or "purchased" or "bought" or "from a flea market, friend or Crank'sList" (or alternatively, when an owner described to me how she got her dog, "stolen" can be another interpretation)
21. "X problem started after (exam) or (new medication you recommended) or (boarding at your facility) or (grooming at your facility) or (nail trim you did), etc."
    Interpretation: "Don't even think about charging me for something that you caused."

As you can see, even when speaking the same language, communication often isn't occurring. In part it's because clients have a different motivation than us, even if it seems like you're both there for the pet. They won't necessarily share that their motivation is to spend as little as possible and be minimally inconvenienced while still trying to appear invested in their pet's health. As I've said before, this isn't *all* clients I'm talking about here. I hate feeling like a lawyer with a hostile witness on the stand, trying to get good and accurate history out of an owner. And they, too, split legal hairs with you over semantics, like Bill Clinton under oath, and lie without blinking an eye. When the lady brings in her nineteen-year-old cat to our practice for the first time, even though she's lived in the same area all that time and she tells you "he hasn't been to a vet in over a year", she's not lying. She's just not telling you the whole truth, which is it hasn't been to any vet in eighteen years, which is certainly "over a year".

In a recent phone conversation with a client, the phrase "unnecessary testing" came up, like a cheese-grater to my ears. When they use this term, what they're really saying is that they've already determined not to do what you're recommending. Or, they did do what you recommended, the results came back negative (ie normal ACTH stim test) and now they get to beat you over the head with the phrase "unnecessary testing". Often, "unnecessary testing" really translates to "unnecessarily opening my pocketbook".

Another misused term is "misdiagnosis". The word gets thrown at us (or maybe just me, I don't know) and I don't think people understand it. If I tell you your dog has feline leukemia, yeah, that's a misdiagnosis. If I tell you your dog has lymphoma and we treat for lymphoma, but it really has bubonic plague, that's a misdiagnosis (as well as a potentially bigger problem). However, if I tell you that your dog *might* have neoplasia as part of the rule-out list and testing reveals, instead, an immune-mediated disease, then...not a misdiagnosis. Having mentioned neoplasia, I also said it may be other things, such as an immune-mediated disease. It doesn't help that some clients have selective hearing. If you run with your dog in the summer, in Texas, during the day, while it has an upper respiratory infection, and its temperature reaches 106.7, I will tell you that is heat stroke. Just because 3 or 4 days later it continues to cough because of the upper respiratory infection which we're treating, doesn't mean your dog was misdiagnosed. If your dog is fine on a visit from 8 months ago, but now has a heart-related condition, that is not a misdiagnosis. That is because the problem wasn't there before, now it is. If I had the ability to see the future, I'd charge more. Finally, if tests haven't come back yet and your pet's condition worsens while getting supportive treatment, that, also, is not a misdiagnosis. That is a "wedon'tyethavea"-diagnosis. There's a difference. If we didn't have to do testing to get a diagnosis, if I had the ability to just look at a pet, or do that "laying on of hands" thing, and tell exactly what something is every time, well, I'd charge more for that too. And then wait to listen to the complaints about costs.

It does make me wonder why people believe medicine is just so easy. As if biological organisms aren't titrating normal parameters within narrow nanogram levels. As if there isn't overlap among disease processes. As if they've never been through any medical process on the human side themselves. I've heard so many stories from the human medicine arena, where they're allowed to do infinitely more than we are, and are left scratching their heads at what could possibly be wrong. And some of these diagnostic gauntlets and/or hospitalizations can go on for months. Without answers. And we have clients who get impatient that it takes a couple of days to get blood work results back, much less results that indicate more will need to be done.

Just think of the amount of time spent trying to pry an accurate answer out of an owner about diet. You can't ask, "Do you feed from the table", because I've had one couple say, "Oh, no, of course not. We put it in a bowl first", completing missing the point of the question. "Do you feed people food?" Seems straight-forward. Yet some people don't interpret that the same way you and I do. Some think that if they cook for their dog, that's the *dog's* food; they don't eat it. Also, some people won't even think of scraps as giving people food. They also won't remember the chips and other items they give the dog throughout the day because it's just a habit and they don't really think of that when you ask. Even if they fess up to giving people food, they will automatically dismiss it as the cause, because they've "always fed him that". Though they have brought their dog in for vomiting and diarrhea. One of my work-arounds with this is, just like us, we can't eat the things that we used to; which I actually believe is true, because most of these are middle-aged dogs and I'm sure their system can't handle the jalapeno pizzas the way it used to. My go-to is to ask what they feed on a normal day. Usually you'll get a straight answer and possibly the truth. If you let an owner talk long enough about what they feed their pet, they'll probably continue to add to the list of things they feed that they didn't include the first time around.

It's important to hear the nuances in Clientese. Because there is a big difference between "vomiting" and "vomited". A big difference between "not eating at all" and "eating less". Even the eating questions will get misinterpreted. One client told us the dog hadn't eaten in three days. After much discussion it was revealed the dog hadn't eaten in three days because the owner had withheld food, not because it was actually inappetent, as we had initially been led to believe. You'll run across a rare client who will get majorly pissed off at being questioned on these distinctions. They don't recognize or they reject their role in providing information to figure out what is wrong. Nothing better than walking into a room and asking, "So what seems to be the problem?" and an owner says, irritated, "You're the doctor! You tell me!" Makes me sigh every time. Because then you have to cajole out of them what prompted them to bring the pet in; as if they didn't know what you meant in the first place. This happens with the vague "not doing right", "not acting right". You have to try to pin this vagueness down by asking, "What is it you're seeing at home or what did you tune into that made you bring him in today?" It often feels we're doing the majority of the work when it comes to these kinds of conversations.

Practice Tips

I know I spoke about it in the foreword, and I often use a lot of tongue-in-cheek when giving advice, but you probably shouldn't really ever take anything I say too seriously. If you've gotten this far, you may have already realized that, if I offer anything, it is the freedom to not take *anything* too seriously. Sometimes, when I say something or present a scenario that I have found funny, I wait for a certain subset of our population to point out or comment how I should be taking such-and-such seriously and this is how they recommend I approach future situations. And yet, all I was doing was presenting one of many absurd situations that happen to us in a particular day. Trust me, you serious-minded people out there, in real-life I certainly do treat clients with the utmost respect, decorum, and empathy. It is not necessary to point out to me how to handle situations because you felt my blasé or sarcastic approach may not be best. I am very aware. I am also very aware of how my brain works and it is impossible for me to ignore and point out the humor in the things we deal with. I find irreverence in most everything and if you've been offended by anything in this book, it was unintended. What is intended is to provoke a little laugh, even if you feel guilty about it, as you may have in the previous Seuss send-up. That is my ultimate goal here.

Which leads me to say, the following Practice Tips, if you wish to implement any in your own practice is completely at your discretion. The reader assumes all of the risks associated with the use and/or implementation of any/all Practice Tips herein. Said reader waives, releases, and discharges the author from any and all liability, including but not limited to death, disability, embarrassment, personal injury, property damage or theft, rashes, blasphemes, or soiling oneself. The reader also indemnifies, holds harmless, and promises not to sue the author should any of the following Practice Tips prove more eventful than intended. Should any Practice Tips result in financial reward to said reader, however, 10% of the proceeds are required to be given to the author as well as a nice 'thank you' note and some nice shrubbery with perhaps a little path running down the middle.

This liability form shall be construed broadly to provide a release and waiver to the maximum extent permissible under applicable law, plus a little bit more.

I CERTIFY THAT I HAVE READ THIS DOCUMENT AND I FULLY UNDERSTAND ITS CONTENT. I AM AWARE THAT THIS IS A RELEASE OF LIABILITY AND A CONTRACT AND I SIGN IT OF MY OWN FREE WILL EVEN THOUGH, BY DEFINITION, I AM A VETERINARIAN, AND THEREFORE NOT OF SOUND MIND OR BODY.

_____   _____   _____
Reader's Name (print as legibly   Date   Reader's Illegible Signature
as possible for a medical professional)

We like to make our practice as pleasant a place as possible. We recognize you have many choices when it comes to choosing who to care for your pet's health. So please feel free to find another place to take your pet. On the other side of this card we have provided a list of other animal hospitals that you could bother, haggle, and/or argue with. Though we appreciate your special pet, we enjoy your absence. Please lose our number. :)

Practice Tip #12: Unwelcome Cards

*****

Practice Tip #25: Handing out marijuana in your waiting room will cut down on client impatience and make the clinic experience more pleasurable

"I find your Collie to be very sexy."

"uh... thanks."

Practice Tip #33: Clients appreciate it when you praise their pets

*****

Practice Tip #39: an unlisted home number is a boon to consecutive hours of sleep

"We need an emergency neuter."

216

Practice Tip #78: Associate vets make great stunt doubles

Mrs. West is coming in at 3:15!

Dr. Lilly, there's a difficult clien...uh, case I'd like you to see at 3:15.

Great!

*****

Practice Tip #87 - Communication: Tact is very important.

How much time does Roscoe have left, Doctor?

Well, let's see.... it's two o'clock now....

"Johnny must have just worn his *little self* out."

Practice Tip #114 — Dealing with children in your clinic: Ketamine 10mg/Kg IM

*****

Yes, the saying is "the customer is always right" ..... but, you're a client.

Practice Tip #129: If you never anger, irritate, or upset a client, you aren't doing your job.

"Oh, how nice. Didn't he play the banjo in 'Deliverance'?

Practice tip #138: Try not to comment on a pet's (or client's) questionable parentage.

*****

Practice Tip #217: Tell clients to put all informative brochures and hand-outs in their bathroom. This way they may actually read them.

Practice Tip #254: Offering anti-inflammatories doesn't make a client less angry

*****

Practice Tip #321: Choose your words carefully

Well, duuuhh!!

"Why can't you be more like your associate, Dr. Smith?"

Practice Tip #357: Treating your staff like family has its limits

*****

"Whew, Franky! That was a pungent one, buddy!"

"Wha?"

Practice Tip #372: You shouldn't fart in the exam room unless you can blame it on the pet.

Practice Tip #403: Listening is a learned art

...yak yak yak yak yak yak yak yak yak yak yak...

...uh huh..... ummmm, I see.... really!?.... uh huh..... yes, yes....

*****

Don't forget to take food away tonight!

—flick!—

Later.....

Why does my ear hurt? Oh! That's right! I need to pick up Stumpy's food!

Practice Tip #411: Earflick owners to emphasize important points, thereby increasing compliance

"This disease's origin dates back to 1818 and was first treated with ingestion of dried Nimbuku leaves. During the late nineteenth century a Russian doctor......"

Practice Tip #980: Be thorough when talking to a client so they can make an informed decision

Veterinary Truisms

What follows here are some of the unspoken rules of veterinary medicine. These are the things that even if they aren't 100% accurate, they're pretty close and certainly have that substantive feel of believability. You won't find these things talked about in other advice arenas, however I believe they're important to acknowledge to make your life easier, if only by a chuckle.

1. An estimate, in the mind of the client, is an exactimate.

2. The person who feeds table scraps or overfeeds the pet will not be the person currently in the exam room with you.

3. If a client has to ask their spouse, the pet's treatment will not happen.

4. You will be held accountable for what you say, what you don't say, how you say it, and what the client thinks you said.

5. The client who is late to their appointment will be in a hurry.

6. The additional pet brought to an exam who is "just along for the ride", isn't.

7. An owner who tells you they will be "waiting by the phone for your call", are "easily reached" at the given number, or "always have my cell phone with me", will not.

8. If you tell a client when test results will be ready, you will be wrong.

9. Always double how long someone tells you their pet has been ill.

10. Anyone who is late to their appointment or know you're near to closing will always be "only five minutes away". Corollary: When they say this, assume they mean football minutes.

11. Clients can relate a problem to anything that was previously done at your clinic regardless of how much time has passed. Example: (problem: ie tumor, coughing, limping, spontaneous combustion, etc.) has been present ever since (spay, nail trim, boarding, driving by the practice, etc.) back last (week, month, year, decade, etc.)

12. People will always double what they say they spent at the vet's compared to what they actually did.

13. If you are told a pet "doesn't like men", you'll find the truth is they don't like anyone.

14. If you have to carry a pet to and/or from a person's car, they will have parked as far from the front door as possible.

15. If the owner is asking if it is ok to give "Substance A" to their pet, they've actually already given it.

16. If you have the most accessible, easy-to-hit, Alaskan pipeline-sized vein, the pet will be the most uncooperative and fractious patient. Conversely, the sweetest, most easily-handled, cooperative pet will have the tiniest hard-to-find vein to hit.

17. The client will tell you the most valuable piece of information in diagnosing their pet while you are using your stethoscope.

18. You will always be told that the poor dog with the smelly, matted, oily, tangled mess of a coat is scheduled for grooming "tomorrow". This will be stated no matter when in the year or how often you see this dog. "Tomorrow" never comes. Addendum: all of the problems with the dog's coat is not what it will be in for.

19. The word "not" is the most widely client-misheard word in a veterinary setting.
    What is said: "This problem will reoccur."
    What is heard: "This problem will not reoccur."
    What is said: "Make sure to not let Bongo run after surgery."
    What is heard: "Make sure to let Bongo run after surgery."

20. Client definition of expensive: it costs something.

21. The Scheduling Paradox: It is not important for clients to be on time, only for you to be on time in seeing clients.

22. There is an inverse relationship between how loudly a client proclaims how well they take care of their pet and how well they actually do.

23. Once a client uses the term "you people", you can be done with the conversation.

24. The best, nicest dogs get the worst diseases.

25. You will know exactly where you stand with a client and what they think of you the first time you tell them "no".

26. If the owner doesn't have previous paperwork and/or can't remember the name of their previous vet, that means they don't exist.

27. Diagnostic Exclusion Principle: If an owner obtains a diagnosis on their pet by looking something up on-line, it will not be that problem. Addendum: If an owner thinks their dog is fat because it *must* be hypothyroid, it won't be. If you've tried and tried for years to get a pet testing for hypothyroidism and the owner finally does, it will be.

28. Veterinary clinics are the only place where shit will literally hit the fan.

29. If you never have a client who is angry or inconvenienced, you aren't doing your job.

Prescriptions

The idea for this section came from the idea "What if we wrote prescription labels not how medication should be given, but by how clients really do give them?" So, following are some of the ones I came up with as seen applied in real life.

We Care More Than The Other Guy Animal Clinic

Dr. Richard Dawson

"Festus" Pinchot   01/21/15

Heartworm Preventative   Qty: 12

Give one tablet whenever
you remember to

Expiration Date: Never   Refill: Never since it lasts forever

*****

Too Precious Peterinary Clinic

Dr. Chuck Barris

"Sylvester" Paddington   04/01/15

Insulin   Qty: 1 bottle

Give as many Units as you think
necessary based on whim and fancy

Expiration Date: When left out of refrigerator   Refill: After hospitalization with diabetic ketoacidosis

AAA Budget Pet Care

Dr. Pat Sajak

"Peter" Parker   01/08/15

Ear Medication   Qty: 1 bottle

Instill as few drops as possible now and then to one or both ears because it's really hard until months from now you get them rechecked

Expiration Date: Never; good   Refill: Whenever
for all subsequent ear problems   you want forever

*****

Jacked-Up Animal Hospital

Dr. Jack Paar

"Hermione" Potter   03/27/15

Eye Medication   Qty: 1 bottle

Get three people to help you hold while you instill 1 - 2 drops in vicinity of eye(s)

Expiration Date: When   Refill: Constantly
turns brown

Cats Only No Dogs Cats Cats Cats Clinic
Dr. Bob Barker

"Tim" Smith   02/12/15

Antibiotic/Steroid Spray   Qty: 1 bottle

Spray affected area once or twice a day for 1 - 14 days or whatever

Can be used for all similar or different skin problems

Expiration Date: Until empty   Refill: Years from above date

*****

Pet Care Is Us
Dr. Bob Eubanks

"Mister" Tibbs   03/15/15

Antibiotics   Qty: 60

Give orally one tablet twice a day unless too difficult

Expiration Date: Still good in cabinet years from now   Refill: Never finish, never need refill

Tweedledee All Pets Hospital
"The Smarter Choice"
Dr. Alex Trebek

"Buster" Brown   06/15/15

Pain Medication   Qty: 60

To save money and not actually treat pain, give 1/2 of recommended dose on occasion.

Expiration Date: Sooner than you will actually stop giving

Refill: Yearly or less

*****

Prestige Animal Hospital, Spa, Refuge, & Resort
Dr. Monty Hall

"Aleksanteri" Ihalainen   31/5/15

Flea Prevention   Qty: 6

Give on rare occasion when your intuition says there might be fleas or relatives are visiting, ignoring what the word prevention means

Expiration Date: Doesn't matter since you'll ignore it anyway

Refill: Never, since it never worked anyway

Generic Corporate Animal Clinic (GCA)

" We care when you don't"

Dr. Steve Harvey

"Barney" Fife 10/26/18

Antibiotics   Quantity: 60

Give in the mouth-hole, which is the front end of the dog, beneath the nose and above the chin. Give every 12 hours (or whenever) for about 2-3 days because it's not better yet.

Expiration Date: Why? You don't look at it anyway.

Refill: unnecessary since you'll have plenty left over

*****

The Gentlest Doctor

" We touch your pets where you can't"

Dr. Chuck Woolery

"Leia" Organa 05/02/18

Seizure Medication   Quantity: 60

Give twice a day until you haven't seen any seizures in a bit, then stop. Don't recheck until seizures have gotten worse or six months, whichever comes first.

Expiration Date: When your pet does

Refill: probably a good idea, except how you use it

What The Hell Is That? Animal Hospital

" You break 'em, We fix 'em"

Dr. Wink Martindale

"Tubby" Teckers   03/18/16

Heart Medication   Quantity: 60

Give twice a day until coughing stops.
Recheck when coughing starts again.
Repeat above as often as necessary.

Expiration Date: Refill: none needed; one "round"
In 5, 4, 3, 2, 1......   should fix problem forever

*****

Petual Healing Animal Hospital

Dr. Peter Marshall

"Dahmer" Bundy   01/18/17

Insulin   Quantity: 1 breakable bottle

Give a few units randomly every day or so.
Hope for the best. Pray.

Expiration Date: Refill: now and then
when you drop it

Bingo

Feeling bored at work? Need something to liven up the day? My expertise is in time-wasting, team-building exercises. I credit my advanced degree in attention-deficit disorder. Below you'll find two bingo cards. The first one is filled out with common things that may occur in a typical day. Mark them off as you encounter them and the first one to get Bingo wins a prize of indeterminate value. The second one is the veterinary conference edition based on the same premise. Going with a group of people? Challenge them to Bingo each and every day. Make sure you have each other's cell phone numbers so you can announce your win wherever you are. After all, are you really paying attention in those classes? Anyway. Enjoy!

Veterinary Bingo

Client late for appointment	Not Neutered (pet, not client)	Anti-vaccines Anti-flea product Anti-heartworm product Anti-pick a med.	The "Oh, wait, one more thing" client	Blood machine error
"My friend/relative is a vet tech"	The "nurse" client	No Lunch Again	Anal gland incident	Muzzling the dog that doesn't ever bite
Fleas: Never had, doesn't have, will never have in future	Real Emergency!	Do It For Free Space	No table food except.....	Have the "your pet is a big fatty-fat" conversation
Prior history paperwork lost or unavailable	Rabies only visit	Client presents lists of internet searches	Working Late	Extra pet brought for appointment
The "just need to talk to Dr. for 5 min." client	The financial-limitations client	"Emergency"	The groomer/breeder/feed store advice	Crazy Client

Veterinary Bingo
Conference Edition

Acronym You Don't Know	See very lonely, forlorn exhibit hall vendor	Get to pet random service or rescue dog	Someone's phone goes off during lecture	Stand in line (for lecture, food, bathroom, etc.)
You find "Free" lunch math daunting	Caught cold and/or flu from fellow primate vector	Successfully navigate exhibit hall without making vendor eye contact	Candy Crush High Score!	Half-way through, realizing you're in the wrong lecture
Learned useful tidbit	Spot early morning jogger	Free Lunch Space	Post-prandial somnolence	Wonder if that old guy is still practicing
Snag favorite seating position	Diagnostic equipment you will never have	Lecture title does not match actual lecture	Speaker's voice so soothing..... ....zzzzzzzzzz	Really good and useful lecture!
Mystifying graph presented	Walking around, you easily make your Fitbit goal	Able to identify purpleocytes and thingamaphages on slide	Fill free bag with free stuff!	Your room is scolded by Fire Marshal

Reverse Clinic Survey

I read so much of how we need to get input (through surveys and such) from clients on what they like, don't like, how to serve them better, etc. (as if they're so shy to share their opinions). And then I read the numerous acts of outright bullying through cowardly and inaccurate reviews and other on-line media platforms against my fellow veterinarians. Not only do we take abuse, but we are told to ask for it as well. Granted, there is also praise to be sent our way and that is appreciated. It's just the negative ones affect us so strongly and we feel helpless because there is literally no way to defend ourselves without inviting more criticism. I have often joked that there should be a site where we can review clients on their ability to care for their pets along with their names and addresses (call it Howl.com) since that's basically what they do with us. It seems only fair and the amount of passive and active neglect we see would probably be astonishing and eye-opening for the majority of people. Though it would also be nice to acknowledge the few amazing clients that truly take care of their pets and work with us to make them better. With this in mind, I came up with the Reverse Clinic Survey (because Client Survey or Pet Owner Survey still made it sound like the veterinarian or the clinic were being evaluated). I used a template from a recommended clinic survey from one of veterinary advice magazines on what we are evaluated on by clients as a basis for this. Feel free to copy and use it at your discretion.

Thank you for choosing our hospital for your pets' medical needs. Since you have filled out our clinic survey, we wanted to provide input to you so that you can provide the best possible experience for us, which in turn will benefit you in receiving the service you deserve. We feel that the care your pet receives is a cooperative endeavor between us and you. We have checked the appropriate boxes below for your consideration.

You showed up on time for your appointment and filled out the appropriate paperwork correctly and efficiently.

◊ Strongly Disagree ◊ Disagree ◊ Neutral ◊ Agree ◊ Strongly Agree

You were pleasant and enjoyable to deal with.

◊ Strongly Disagree ◊ Disagree ◊ Neutral ◊ Agree ◊ Strongly Agree

You and your pet responded appropriately and were accommodating during your wait.

◊ Strongly Disagree ◊ Disagree ◊ Neutral ◊ Agree ◊ Strongly Agree

You kept your children quiet and under control during your visit.

◊ Strongly Disagree ◊ Disagree ◊ Neutral ◊ Agree ◊ Strongly Agree

◊ Not applicable

You provided an appropriate carrier, leash, or other restraint device for your pet and/or child for your visit.

◊ Strongly Disagree ◊ Disagree ◊ Neutral ◊ Agree ◊ Strongly Agree

You provided a good history and were clear as to your needs with the receptionists, technicians, and veterinarian.

◊ Strongly Disagree ◊ Disagree ◊ Neutral ◊ Agree ◊ Strongly Agree

You asked relevant questions and remained on-topic regarding your pet's health issues.

◇ Strongly Disagree ◇ Disagree ◇ Neutral ◇ Agree ◇ Strongly Agree

You did not balk at or hinder at the agreed upon diagnostics or treatments.

◇ Strongly Disagree ◇ Disagree ◇ Neutral ◇ Agree ◇ Strongly Agree

In our opinion we felt the payment we received was worth having you visit.

◇ Strongly Disagree ◇ Disagree ◇ Neutral ◇ Agree ◇ Strongly Agree

We would recommend you to other veterinarians based on your visit.

◇ Strongly Disagree ◇ Disagree ◇ Neutral ◇ Agree ◇ Strongly Agree

Jaded Vet Quiz

It's said that it's not the years, it's the mileage. So, though you may know how many chronological years you've been in the profession, where do you fall on the mileage? That what the new Jaded Vet Quiz seeks to determine. Below are ten questions that, depending on your answers, will tell you where you are in your career. Keep track of your answers and add up your points at the end. You may be surprised. Then, again, maybe not. Also, you may want to take this quiz before and after reading this book to see what happens with your score.

1. Eight-year-old, spayed female pitbull comes in for coughing and is diagnosed heartworm positive. The client says how much the LOVE their dog and they have had her their whole life. What do you think the client will do?
a) pursue heartworm treatment
b) "think about treating" after being given an estimate
c) euthanize
d) leave with handouts and never return

2. You have an important family event to attend after work. At a half-hour before closing, a client, who is notorious for being late to appointments, has just called and said they're only "five minutes away" and their pet is very sick. You…….
a) tell them you'll be there and stay late if necessary to get their pet taken care of
b) tell them to come on in, after all, they're only five minutes away and you should have plenty of time to still take care of the problem
c) explain to them that due to the lateness of the day, they would be better off just heading to the nearest emergency clinic
d) notice the caller ID and pretend you're the answering machine

3. The car you drive is:
a) the same one you drove in school
b) the same one you drove in school
c) the same one you drove in school
d) less than ten years old

4. A new client presents their nine-year-old male, neutered, adorable Shih-tzu with coughing, sneezing, diarrhea, anorexia, vomiting, limping, pruritus, and bilateral ear infections. They really want to pursue treatment and make everything better but are limited on funds and aren't qualified for CareCredit. When they ask if they can post-date checks for the next five weeks, you respond:
a) Yes, of course! Whatever it takes to make sure the pet gets treated.
b) Have the dog signed over to you and take responsibility for treatment.
c) Treat what you can for what they're able to afford.
d) Not pursue diagnostics or treatments until they can pay in full.

5. During your veterinary career you have had to call the police to your clinic:
a) zero times
b) once
c) 2 – 5 times
d) more than 5

6. A client is arguing with you and says, "I'm not a veterinarian……" What word or phrase follows?
a) You can't get past understanding why a client would be arguing with you in the first place.
b) Sounds like a complete sentence to me.
c) "but"
d) You don't know, because you've interrupted them before they can finish and say, "That's right."

7. A potentially complicated case is presented to you. What do you expect to happen?
a) You're sure you can get a diagnosis since you know you can explain the severity of the situation and explain things to the client well enough that they will let you do everything you need to do.
b) You chuckle knowingly at a)
c) The client agrees to let you do one test.
d) The clients wants to just give medications and treat symptomatically.

8. In giving information to an owner about a given disease process……
a) In trying to be as thorough as possible you schedule a special time to go over in detail the treatment process, expectations both short-term and long-term, have handouts for the owner, make sure all their questions are answered, have your staff repeat the information to them, schedule recalls and rechecks, and emphasize for them to call with any other concerns or questions as things progress.
b) You tell the owner the basics of the problem, treatment options and what to expect, have your technician review the plan with them, and tell the owner to schedule rechecks.
c) You describe the problem, potential diagnostics and treatments in the simplest, easiest way possible.
d) In trying not to be sued you do as a) above.

9. After you have spent a great deal of time in educating the owner on the problem, which of the following happens?
a) The client has good follow-up questions that allow you to promote their understanding better and they thank you for all of your time and start treatment immediately.
b) Clients says they will start treatment.
c) Client goes on the internet and wants you to answer why you didn't offer the parsley-tumeric treatment which is cheaper and has no side-effects.
d) Client only has one question: "How much is it going to cost?"

10. What best describes your approach to medical situations throughout a day?
a) You reference your books for just about every case and write up a very complete differential list for each problem.
b) You reference your books for complicated cases only.
c) What books?
d) You reference constantly because you realize you've forgotten more than you'll ever know.

Every a) answer is 1 point. Every b) answer is 2 points. Every c) answer is 3 points. Every d) answer is 4 points. No, there is no CE for this quiz. See where you rank below:
10 points: 1st year out of school
11-20 points: 2-10 years out of school
21-30 points: mid-career nervous breakdown
31-39 points: one day at a time
40 points: time to retire

Computer/Schedule Entries

During our day-to-day activities we use a lot of short-hand things to simplify our lives – acronyms, abbreviations, etc. We do this when writing in files when taking histories or putting down our diagnostic findings. Some computer programs, for instance, may only allow you a certain number of characters to input in the problem line when making appointments. If an owner is going on and on with description after exhaustive description of what's wrong with the pet, we may, perhaps, end up putting just ADR (ain't doin' right) or NDR (not doin' right – what I've been told is the northern version of ADR). The person writing or inputting such short-cuts know what they're trying to say, and why, yet others reading the entries later may interpret a completely different slant. These are some of the file entries that I've come across over time and what my brain thought when I saw them.

Sneezing puppies – Sure you may assume the obvious, but it could be that the dog has so many in the litter that they're coming out her nose. I envision little adorable puppies covered in boogers.

Vaccinate left eye – Well, ok. If that's what the owner wants. Hold reeaaallly still, Max.

Coughing bloody black stools – It's bad enough when that's what's coming out the expected end. It's a whole different level coming out the front end!

Not eating diarrhea – Yeah? Well, I wouldn't eat it either!

Lethargic mucousy stool – Awwwww……poor little stool. What's got you down?

Vomiting orange for two days – Sounds like we'll need to do a gastrotomy to get that orange out.

Diarrhea for 34 days – Wow. That's pretty specific. Makes you wonder why their tolerance level for the diarrhea lasted past, oh, I don't know, 3 – 4 days tops!

Limping on leg – As opposed to limping on……..what?

Check ears not acting right – How are ears supposed to act? Now, the left ear isn't supposed to be acting right, that's the right ear's responsibility. So….that makes sense to me, but this distinctly says both ears, so I have no clue. We may need a behaviorist.

Check fatty lump – You have to love the pre-diagnosis appointments. What are you supposed to do with these? "Yep, that's a fatty lump. Next?"

Sneezing watery eyes – I was really curious to see this one. I mainly wanted to see if it was possible for the nostrils to stay open when the eyes sneezed.

Limping lumps – Sure, it could be two different problems, but that's not how it reads. So, these lumps? They have legs? They're hurt?

Check ears and leg – owner reports fell off couch – Wait. What? The ears fell off the couch or the leg? Or was it the owner? And if so, why would they tell us that?

New client fecal – Uh. You can take that bit of nastiness to your own physician, dude.

Rash on skin not acting right – Well, yeah. Rashes, by definition, aren't supposed to act right. They're…….rash. How do you expect it to act?

Can't stand not eating – Me neither. In fact, I'm suddenly hungry.

Check ears excessive drooling – When ears "drool" we call that "bad".

Check eye constipated – It's just seen too much!

Coughing check ears – Well, I don't know what vet school you went to, but I usually listen to the chest if there's coughing. I think that one was a trick question.

Owner needs sedation – Now you might think that this was an incomplete entry and that the owner needs sedation "for their pet", however it could just mean what it says, in which case I'm thinking something intramuscular.

New puppy seeing worms – Is anyone else seeing these worms? Is the puppy hallucinating?

Running nose – Go, nose, go!

New client scratching – Oh, it's you again. Look, we only see animals here. And would you stop doing that in the lobby and please leave!

Limping hot spots – I'm thinking this one goes along with the limping lumps. I've started using this as one of those things Robin was always saying: "Limping Hot Spots, Batman!"

Falls over for no reason – Oh, he has a reason, I'm sure.

Coughing AF – This one made me pause before I realized it wasn't the impolite 21st century abbreviation meaning "extremely" or "very" but was the tech's initials.

Needs vaccines MF – Again, tech's initials, but at first I was extremely motivated to get in there and do those vaccines!

Typos can be fun as well. While still working on this blog an appointment was made to "Check Sin". There are seven differentials for that: Sloth, Greed, Gluttony, Envy, Lust, Wrath, and Dopey. One last thing. We use a lot of acronyms in this profession, both for describing diseases and as file entry short-hand. There's one I'd like for us to get away from and that one is this: FU. It's supposed to mean Follow-Up, but, ya know, when you see it, that's not the first thing that pops into your head. The first time I was exposed to this particular bit of short-hand it was on a sticky note stuck to a chart: **FU Dr. Docsway**   *What'd I do?*

Pet Names

Anyone else have a problem when you get the owner's name confused with the pet's name because the owner's first name seems like it should be the pet's name? It doesn't happen often, but recently we had an owner whose name was "Tikelia" (pronounced Tequila). When you are just skimming the file folder before walking into the room, I think you should be excused for calling the dog by the owner's name. Especially when you do it really enthusiastically, like, "Hey, Tikelia! How ya doing? Who's a good dog?! Who's a good dog?!" Right? Does this happen to anyone else? Anyone? Fine. Maybe it's just me.

I had two encounters with those people who like to alter a pet's name just to give others a hard time when it's mispronounced. In your mind think about how most anyone normal would pronounce "Sheba". Hint: "Shee-ba". Got it fixed in your head? Okay. After I called out for "Sheba" to come into the exam room, I was corrected with just that right amount of archness and condescension, "It's pronounced Sheb-ah!" The "e" being a short-"e" sound, unlike the socially understood and accepted long-"e" sound. Then there was the Chihuahua named "Katty", which I thought was one of those too-cute things where we name them after a different species, like the cat we have named "Dog". After calling them to the room, I was informed that it's pronounced "Katy", to which I couldn't help but say, "Well, if you'd dropped one of the "T"s, I would have gotten it right." These kinds of interactions make it certain that I will never say the pet's name ever again; I will only refer to them as him or her, he or she. And then get corrected when I mess up the pronouns. And when that happens my default response is, "Hey, I just barely got people's genders figured out."

I'd like to throw a little sympathy toward our front-line receptionists who have to put up with the brunt of silly and frustrating client interactions. What is it with people, for instance, when asked for their last name in an attempt to pull or access their file, who reply with: "My last name or my dog's last name?" Does your dog have its own last name? Is it like a step-dog where the last name would be different? Does it have a middle name too, so that when you're really angry at it you'll yell, "Eileen Luann Smith, you stop sniffing that other dog's butt right now!" What do they think we mean? Yes, ma'am, *your* last name. You filled out the client information form that generated the file. Your dog doesn't have its own legal name enabling it to go independently open a savings account, buy a car, or file separation procedures with a lawyer to get away from your craziness.

Speaking of last names, here are some pet names that combine in funny ways with owner's last names and what they make me think when I hear them:

Chip Chipman – this is the hero's earnest and plucky sidekick in any 1950s screwball comedy

Oreo Imburgia – the condition you get when you've eaten way too many Oreos, the symptoms of which include, but are not limited to: borborygmus, abdominal distension, and melena.

Oops Jordan – Michael's less talented cousin

Harmony Hall – unlike Carnegie it's a lot easier to get into this hall

Monkee Baker – either an occupation taken by a member of the Monkees after their fame waned or a chain of primate-based pastry stores regularly picketed by PETA

Mercedes Hardcastle – a short-lived 1980s female private detective show: "Mercedes Hardcastle P.I." There was a running gag about her moustache.

Dinky Abbot – world's tallest monk; the local bishop was the one who coined his nickname, which caused him to be forever stuck being called Brother Dinky

Puss N Boots Gamble – the Gambles, of Proctor and Gamble, who left all of their fortune to their cat who now has closets and closets-full of footwear

Honey Walker and **Texas Walker** – the next President of the United States and the First Husband

Dusty Rossi – Carlo's brother who's winery specializes in really, really, really dry white wines

Puff McLeish – a laid-back non-threatening Irish drug dealer

Finally there's Mr. and Mrs. Cummings and their dog "Squirt". I'll let you do the work on this one. Honestly, I'm not commenting on it, but come on owners! Really?! You didn't think this out did you? *sigh* I'm going to some place a lot warmer than Florida for including this one!

Then there are the pets whose names become more interesting when they have a particular problem. I think we've all had or known the diabetic pet named "Sugar". For variety there's the diabetic dog named "River". Irony combined with PU/PD! Recently had a dachshund named Skippy, who wasn't really that skippy when he came in with intervertebral disc disease.

Anyone out there been bit by "Karma"? In the literal sense, that is. And what about the two cats, "Booger" and "Sniffles" with upper respiratory infections? Did the owners *know* that these guys were going to be so afflicted in their lives and that's why they named them or did the mere act of naming them cause the disease process? Starts to sound like the names for the Seven Dwarves – "Sneezy", "Booger", "Sniffles", "Wheezy", "Snotty", "Sinusitis", and me, "Doc". Then there's the epileptic dog named "Spaz". It's almost too easy. I'm proud to say that I am assured getting into heaven because I can truthfully say I neutered "Satan". Though I euthanized "Jesus" also, so it might be a wash. Then there's "Mr. Biggles" and "Miss Bailey" who, apparently, are unashamedly living together in sin. We can only hope that "Mr. Biggles" will do the right thing and one day make an honest woman of "Miss Bailey". My favorite, though, has to have been "Braveheart" who had gotten to the age that he needed to be on NSAIDs pretty regularly. All I could picture was an aged Mel Gibson with a Scottish brogue: "You can take our lives! But you can't take our……Aaaarrgghh! Ow! My back! Oh, god, my back's gone out! Someone help me up here!"

Finally, there was the cat named "Guess".
"What's your cat's name?"
"Guess."
"Um. Ok. Is it Callie?"
"No. Guess!"
"Kitty?"
"No! Guess!"
"Genoa Buttercups Toilwinovitz?"
sigh

Pet Names Part 2

We've all had our share of Labradors named Max, Beagles named Shiloh, Chow Chows named Bear, and white Persians (or anything else white and fluffy) named Snowball. I'm not here to talk about them. Instead, I'd like to talk about the random thoughts that cross my mind in regards to pet names. Now, since I'm more of a dog and cat veterinarian, this discourse will be a little skewed. Certainly, if anyone out there has thoughts and experience in naming iguanas, horses, or ficus, feel free to drop me a line.

I find the naming of dogs based on their historical background a bit dubious and unquestionably overdone. For instance, after all of the Chicos, Diegos, and Pacos, I'd really like to meet a Chihuahua named Bob. Just Bob. That would be refreshing. And what about German Shepherds named Hans, Rommel, and Wolfgang? Are such names supposed to remind people or the dog about their heritage? In that case, some good names for a Polish Tatra Sheepdog could be Kowalski, Łukaszewicz, or Młynarczyk. It just seems redundant. How about a German Shepherd named Pedro? See, that works for me. Nothing like some cognitive dissonance in a name.

And what about naming pets based on their supposed profession. I speak, of course, about Boxers named Tyson. Please stop. Come on, folks, some originality! If you absolutely *must,* due to some deep-seated compulsion, how about showing some regard for notables such as Braddock, Marciano, or Carter? Isn't it funny how no one names female Boxers after......oh, I don't know, female boxers? There's a 1980s female featherweight champion with the last name Canino. It doesn't get much more perfect than that. I'd like to see someone name their Pug after a famous boxer since the original term used for the sport was pugilism. That I could respect. Since we're on the subject, why aren't there more Portuguese Waterdogs or any other water-sport breed for that matter, named Lougainis, Phelps, or Thorpe?

Also, naming big dogs things like Tiny or Peewee.........no. First of all, it's only cute as a thought. Secondly, owners need to realize that these dogs will get their revenge, much like the Boy Named Sue did in the Johnny Cash song. And the opposite, such as Yorkies named Rambo, must be stopped. These poor guys have to put up with all of those sarcastic comments down at the groomer's such as, "Oooooooo......watch out! Here comes Rambo!" or "Oh, please don't eviscerate me, *Rambo,* you might get blood on your little *hair-bow!*"

People need to get over trying too hard to give their pets original names. This disease has sloughed over from people naming their children something "original" only to find out that there are now three "Jenyfurr"s in their third-grade class. If you are going to go out of your way to make a name difficult, at least have some patience with clinic staff when you tell them your pet's name is "Murphy" and they don't automatically know to spell it as "Murffie". Yelling at someone misspelling your dog's unusually spelled name is only a good way to be instantly remembered when making appointments later. Considering the pet's name is not on an official document such as a driver's license or paycheck, please realize that it will still respond to its name no matter how it is written in the chart. I think the most ridiculous one that presented to me was the owner who was filling out surgical paperwork for their pet, Bandit, and felt the need to add another "T" at the end wherever their pet's name appeared.

I also get a laugh out of names that coincidentally relate to why they are in. For instance, the dog named Skippy with a torn cruciate (different dog than the IVDD mentioned earlier). The hit-by-car dog whose name happened to be Crash (this is only funny because Crash was a Saint Bernard who was unhurt which could not be said for the vehicle that hit him). Then there was the dog named Ali who had a taken a beating in a dog fight. Or the Persian named Stertor who presented with breathing difficulties. Ok......I made that last one up. But, it would be funny.

Finally, let's talk about the funny combinations that occur when people don't consider how the pet's name and the owner's last name will sound together. Below are some of my favorites and what they make me think of every time I hear them.

Fuzzy Irving – a drink you can get during any Happy Hour at a literary pub

Monkey Hall – Congress

Kitty Pickett – a dog protest line when an owner tries to introduce a cat to the house

Sissy Pope – a Catholic leader so ineffectual his name was removed from history

Oreo Fightmaster – the winner of the television show that pits Ultimate Fighter contestants versus HGTV's Ace of Cakes

Midnight Filer – a really dedicated employee

Buddha Foreman – the guy who keeps all the other monks in line

Monkey Summers – the next much-anticipated Garrison Keillor novel

Kitty Mace – what a cat uses when getting across the kitty picket line

Bandit(t) Law – general lawlessness of the old West when dogs were dogs and cats were nervous

Cricket Bell – what Pinocchio put on Jiminy so he wouldn't step on him by accident

Monty Blasband – a disease found only in England that is too horrible to describe

Mocha Storm – a new Starbuck's beverage

Floppy LaFave – world's worst gigolo

Peanut Justice – hero to legumes everywhere

Twinkie Swindle – Bernie Madoff's first Ponzi scheme attempt in fourth grade

Has anyone else noticed that the best way to make a dog or cat the meanest and most fractious pet you'll ever see is by naming it "Precious"?

Client Comments

To a large degree I consider the comments below to be instructive, as I think you should be exposed to those things that you least expect people to say and be prepared for the unexpected. I think it also helps, as you'll see in the examples, to see where clients will completely mishear you. These are the things they don't teach you in school. As the years go on, I find myself unsurprised by anything people say. In some cases, in bold, I've put possible answers to these comments.

1. "Rice stops itching."
2. "Can you declaw just one paw?" **Is he only right-pawed?**
3. "Huskies don't get fleas."
4. "How much is a quarter cup of food?"
5. "I have a large-medium to large-small sized dog."
6. "She's okay until she bites."
7. "Can you spay them while they're in heat? I've heard that it messes up their hormones and changes their personality."
8. Upon watching a Schirmer tear test being done: "Will that measure how much alcohol he's had?"
9. "I sewed it up with dental floss but it didn't hold." **No way! Really? It didn't work?**
10. "How much will it cost to file down my dog's teeth. My Rottweiler is becoming aggressive and bites my Golden and I don't like that."
11. "If I have a dog and it's always been an outside dog, and you make him an inside dog, will that make him die? My boyfriend's book says so."
12. "My cat is eating extra food and because of this is fat. What can I do?"
13. Told to groomer: "He don't bite until you brush him."
14. First question when answering the phone: "How can I tell if my dog is dead?" **The long-form to this was my office manager going through a list of ways from poking at the dog, yelling its name, putting a mirror up to its nose, etc. For a dog that hadn't moved or responded in three days. They were worried about burying him if he was only mostly dead. I figured if the first shovel-full of dirt in his face didn't startle him, then yeah, probably proper to bury.**
15. "If I buy a prairie dog, will I be allergic to it like I am dogs and cats? Is it like a small dog?"
16. "My dog has been run over in front of my house. How can I tell what it died from and how long ago it died?"
17. On the phone: "I won't be able to pay you, because I'm only five feet tall and my husband left the charge card on top of the tv and I can't reach it." **The winner of the Best Excuse Not To Pay award.**

18. "I've been using my herpes medication on the dog's skin, but it isn't working." **Thanks for sharing more than I wanted to know.**
19. "I didn't know I'd have to wait if I just walked in."
20. "I can tell when he gets bad breath his anal glands need to be done."
21. "I wouldn't have had him neutered if I'd known you were going to remove his testicles."
22. "Do you guys ever wear your dog's collar? I do. He has a spiked collar and when I put it on he gets really upset. It's funny. You should see him."
23. "Can I use Compound W on my dog?"
24. "As they breed dogs smaller and smaller, their hearts stay the same size. My Pomeranians have hearts the same size as a fifty pound dog." **No, that's called chronic heart disease.**
25. "Rabies vaccines cause dogs to become aggressive."
26. "I don't want to neuter my dog, but I don't want to have puppies. Is there a place where I can take him where he can get his freak on. You know, like a doggie whorehouse?"
27. "I vaccinated the father, so I figured the puppies would be protected from parvo."
28. "Well, I don't see why we need to check the other dogs in my house for hookworms, they aren't related to this one anyway!"
29. "I don't need to do presurgical bloodwork because my dog is a purebreed."
30. "When a dog's healthy they stand on their toes." **As opposed to stiffly on their side, I guess.**
31. "He always drinks a lot of water when his ears are bothering him."
32. "I have a cat at home. She's eating and acting fine. But, her butt fell out. Can I get an estimate to fix it?" **"Well, let's see. Butt fell out….butt fell out. Oh, yes! Here it is! $3,000. However, if you actually bring it in it'll probably be lower. The price. Not the butt."**
33. On a follow-up phone call, when asking the owner how their dog is doing, she replied, "Well, I have no idea, he's downstairs!" **"Ma'am, are you safe? Is there a reason you can't go downstairs? Are you locked in the attic and being held captive?"**
34. Owner of a cryptorchid dog: "He has a lump up on his back. I think that's the other testicle." **"That would be something, wouldn't it?"**
35. "I break up the Heartgard into fourths and give 1/4 each day, because they're so big and he can't eat all of it."
36. "She's blind in the right eye and can't see out of the left eye."
37. "Are you telling me that you aren't going to allow me to take the medication home unless I pay for it first?"
38. "He's only chewing where his skin meets the foot."
39. "I deal with his hip problem by taping his legs together with masking tape. He seems to enjoy it."

40. "Ivermectin and Geritol is a home remedy for heartworms."
41. "Dogs with double back dewclaws are immune to rabies."
42. "I deworm my horses and since the dogs eat the horse manure that's how they get dewormed."
43. "Besides having contact with a male, is there any other way my cat could have gotten pregnant?" **"Is your cat named Mary? Have there been any alien abductions in your neighborhood?"**
44. "My dog was poisoned but we treated him with steak and ice cubes and he got better."
45. "My dawg had the internal sickness."
46. "He's been known to snap on occasion, but he doesn't bite."
47. "If you never feed beef to your dog from day one, you will never have fleas."
48. "Can you cut the toenail to get a blood sample to tell how old he is?"
49. "I'm deathly afraid of dogs. The only way I can deal with my own dog is to pretend he's a cat."
50. "My dog is vomiting. Does that mean she's pregnant?"
51. "He's not really that sick. He's just vomiting 3 – 5 times a day."
52. "I want my dog tested for rabies." **"Ok. Let's get him up here on the table. But, you're going to have to stand back for this next part."**
53. "My dog keeps spitting out the Frontline."
54. "Can I give my dog breast milk?"
55. "I only want to buy a half a can."
56. "My dog is 1/2 English Setter, 1/2 Boxer, 1/8 Pitbull, and 1/8 Bulldog."
57. "My cat has been sneezing and having goopy eyes. I didn't bring him in because I know you can't give him antibiotics when they still have retained baby teeth."
58. Breeder about his latest female dog: "Well, I know she's pregnant because I helped."
59. "I think I need to bring my dogs in. She was in heat and they've been stuck together for three weeks now."
60. Written on a note for what the owner wants done to their pet: Shots, check poop, nudder.
61. "I only want my dog to be given 1/2 cc of the rabies vaccine because he's smaller."
62. "We don't trim the hair back that covers his eyes because if we do the light will be too bright and blind him."
63. "We keep him muzzled because it keeps him from peeing and pooping in the house."
64. "My own dog, Abby, is dead, but I have a prescription for her for prednisone where I can get 5 refills. My son's dog has a skin problem, so I want to refill Abby's prednisone for him."
65. "My kitten was born in May and is now seven months old. She was spayed in February."
66. "Well, he's not a morning dog."

67. "My dog's kneecap fell off over the weekend and won't go back on." **"Did you try dental floss?"**
68. "The mother has never had fleas, but her puppies were born with them."
69. "My friend told me to take crushed up seashells and sprinkle it throughout my yard. When the fleas walk on them their own shells break and they'll all die……………………It didn't work."
70. "I was afraid to take away food because if it kept trying to poop without having eaten I was afraid it would poop out its intestines instead."
71. "After I bathe the dog, I sit on the floor naked, and lay the dog across my private parts. If the hair dryer is too warm on my leg then I know it's too hot to use on him." **And this is why I'll never get the image of this old, old lady out of my head.**
72. Dog with inguinal hernias: "The steroid injections make those lumps go away."
73. Conversation between clients when being instructed on giving insulin: Husband: "Can we reuse the syringes?" Wife: "No, you idiot! You want him to get AIDS?!"
74. After recommending neutering: "Then what would he lick back there?"
75. "Can dogs use tampons?" **"Only as foreign bodies."**
76. "I'm not consistent with the heartworm prevention. But, I don't have to be because I live on the eleventh floor."
77. "When you board cats, how do they go to the bathroom?"
78. "I think my cat has diabetes, because it has a fungal infection around his anus."
79. "My neighbor gave her dog a shot of the distemper/parvo and three days later he was foaming at the mouth and died. I think he already had parvo, so when she gave him the shot, he got double-parvo."
80. "If I refer people to your clinic do I get something?"
81. **"If my little dog eats my other dog's large breed food, will it hurt him?**
82. "I don't need any heartworm prevention because I have a fenced yard."
83. "We add bleach to the water when we bathe our Westie so he stays white." **"Nooooooo…"**
84. "You need to give me a handicapped permit for my car since my dog had knee surgery."
85. The owner referring to their own German Shepherd: "Well, of course he bites. They know when you are doing silly things. They're very smart dogs and they're just correcting silly behaviors. We get corrected all the time!"
86. "Well, I sleep a lot, so I don't know whether he's eatin' or drinkin'."
87. "I want one of them there GPS tracking devices for dogs. I don't want it for my dog, though. I have a bunch of rental properties and I want to put those things in the refrigerator, so when people steal 'em I can track 'em down."
88. After explaining what can be expected with the owner's dog giving birth: "You mean there's going to be a mess?"

89. "I think her back is broken." **Cat was found to be in heat**

90. After being told the client will need to speak to the doctor: "I don't see the point in talking with her again since she won't agree with me!"

91. "When our declawed cat has it's kittens, will the kittens have claws?"

92. "I knew something was wrong with my dog when I came home and he did not hump my leg as hard as he normally does."

93. "It says here he got the D..A...P..P...C....somethin' but it also says it was killed, so whatever he had they killed it, so that's good."

94. "Well, I don't want to spend anything. That's why I'm on the phone, so you can just tell me what I need to do."

95. "I'm not worried about the seizures he's having because he's inbred."

96. "Can I get parvo if my dog bites me?"

97. Condensed conversation (actually took about 20 minutes on the phone): "I want to get those yeast pills! I know my dog has yeast because he's peeing everywhere! I think he got the yeast problem because he eats so much damn bread! He loves that damn bread! You want me to get urine? How am I supposed to get urine out of him?!"

98. Concerning a spay: "Is that procedure reversible?"

99. On the phone: "I want to know if you'll take Medicaid for my dog?"

100. "Can she sleep after she has the subQ fluids?"

101. "Can you give bleach internal for a dog with Parvo?"

102. "What can I use from home to deworm my kitten?"

103. "Can you do surgery to bring a dog's breasts up after giving birth?"

104. "If my dog died of Parvo, can my kitten get it?"

105. "If your dog gets the mange, he'll go crazy!"

106. "What's that flea control stuff that goes straight to a dog's brain and kills 'em?"

107. "Does my Rotti have Parvo again?"

108. "Can I do anything for my dog when he's sick instead of bringing him to the vet?"

109. On the phone: "I really don't have any money right now, but my cat has something wrong with its leg. Can I just email you a picture of it instead so you can tell me what's wrong and how to fix it?"

110. "Our dog died sometime yesterday and we were wondering if you could tell us how to perform our own autopsy at home? We were unable to find any directions on the internet."

111. After telling the owner that their Boxer has a heart murmur: "Oh, no! Not one of those Generic things!" **"Or 'genetic'. Whichever."**

112. "The label says to put one drop in both eyes. And I've really tried! But no matter what I try I can't do just half-a-drop!"

113. On the answering machine: "I'm pissed off! I tried to pick up my dog after you closed and no one was there to help me!" **This was a client who we'd tried to contact all day long. Even stayed about 20 minutes after closing. The dog was fine. Owner left the message an hour and a half after closing.**

114. On the phone: "I need to reschedule my appointment. I don't know what I'm coming in for. You'd have to talk to that lady I made the appointment with the first time. She'd know why I'm coming in!"

115. "My dog ate cat poop. How do I adjust his insulin dosage to account for that?"

116. "She craps all over the place and her butt smells. I guess she's preparing me to have a husband."

117. "Does dewormer make a dog's butt smell?"

118. "The Omega Fatty Acid pills you gave me don't work because I haven't been able to give them to him."

119. "Wow! You're quick! He bit the crap out of the last vet we saw."

120. "Why are my cats gay?"

121. "You can smell that it's mange."

122. "We know he doesn't have fleas because he drinks out of the pool."

123. "Will my Red Bone Hound become a Lab if she nurses her part-Lab puppies?"

124. "After you cut my dog's nails, can you put them into a plastic bag for me to keep?"

125. "Why is my dog vomiting after eating horse manure?" **"Must not have been high-quality horse manure."**

126. "Heartworms are just something vets made up to make money."

127. "Corn in the dog food makes your dog go crazy!"

128. "I have a pedophile to do my dog's nails." **"That's awfully nice of them."**

129. "She's an indoor dog, but I keep her outside."

130. In regards to an extremely rotund Australian Shepherd: "Everyone keeps telling us she's fat, but the way we figure it, she's the right weight for her breed, but she just has a smaller frame."

131. During a recheck, asking owner if they were able to get the medicine in the dog's ears: "No, I don't think so. Why?"

132. "I only want a partial dental."

133. Upon calling a client who was late to their appointment, the client replied: "We cancelled our appointment, but forgot to call and tell you."

134. "I don't believe in rabies." **"Rabies is kind of like God. It believes in you."**

135. "When dogs get their butts stuck together, does that mean they're 100% pregnant?"

136. Reason given for visit: "My cat is ungrateful." **"Pretty much the definition of 'cat'."**

137. "I read that dogs eat dirt if they're anemic. So, if he's anemic should I feed him dirt?"

138. Client on phone with dog with obvious ear hematoma: "My dog's ear is swollen and he needs antibiotics. I don't have any money to bring him in for something so simple since I can lance it myself to let the pus out."

139. "Will Lasix make things work better when it wrings the fluid out of the lungs?"

140. Question of if their dog is having any problems is answered by client: "He steals broccoli." **"You would think if he's going to steal, he'd steal something more useful."**

141. "My dog fell off the bed and his tumor got bigger."

142. In regards to a technician's comment when checking a patient in: "Don't say "surgery" around him because he'll be devastated."

143. "She has bad teeth because she had babies."

144. "I don't give them shots because I don't breed them anymore."

145. "Anesthesia just ruined my dog's coat."

146. "If I feed him the large breed food, will he get bigger?"

147. "My dog just got hit by a car. Can I make an appointment for Saturday at 10 AM?"

148. "I can't believe you put in sutures that my dog could get out!"

149. Problem a cat is brought in for: "He's sleeping a lot."

150. First time Boston Terrier puppy owners: "We're concerned because he seems to have a hard time breathing!"

151. "The flea prevention you sold me gave my dog fleas!"

152. Owner phone call, having bought an Early Pregnancy Test (EPT) for her dog; her question did not relay to the appropriateness of using the test but rather: "I can't figure out how to get her to pee on the stick!" **"Wait, wait. Let me answer this one. Give me the phone! Oh, come on! I want to walk her through it!"**

153. "I cannot believe you sent me a welcome card! I am not a new client there and my dog is not a new patient! I simply brought him there for a second opinion and I want all of my and his information deleted from your system!"

154. "I don't need one of those self-cleaning cat litterboxes. I have a dog that takes care of that."

155. "Papillions are not susceptible to getting fleas."

156. "I don't think he has that dry eye thing you talked about. I think my other dog licks at his eyes and makes them dry."

157. Client on the phone with a very important question: "Is it okay to bathe my dog after he's been run over?"

158. The answer by a client on the phone when asked what problem their dog was having: "He can't exhale."

159. Upon finding out the unspayed female dog is pregnant by the unneutered male in the same household: "I told them not to have sex!"
160. In response to overtly jaundiced urine: "I thought it was due to giving him Gatorade."
161. "She's not current on vaccines, but she has been in the past."
162. "My dog got spayed and she still has fleas. For all I spend on surgery, why does she still have fleas?!"
163. The "It's Your Fault" defense when the dog comes up heartworm positive: "I had to get my heartworm prevention elsewhere. Your prices are so high I couldn't keep her on it!"
164. Winner of the best alternative and useless heartworm treatment: "Feed an avocado and two cigarettes to the dog one month apart." **"Questions. Avocado with the skin? This also doesn't seem very accurate dosing. Is it two cigarettes regardless of size of the dog?"**
165. When asked if any problems giving the medication: "Sometimes I fall asleep and I don't wake up."
166. Regarding doing x-rays to count puppies: "We don't believe in exposing them to radiation. Besides you know how many puppies they'll have by how many nipples swell up."
167. Frustrated about the length of time it's taken to fix a problem an owner gets sayings confused. He thinks about using "nip it in the bud", "kick its butt", and "lick the problem", but what he ends up saying is "I want to lick this problem in the butt!" **"Aren't you just the little go-getter, then? Good for you!"**
168. "Her last heat? I don't know. Don't you think that's kind of personal?"
169. "I don't need heartworm preventative because I rub dryer sheets on my dogs before they go outside."
170. "It's been ten months and we know she should have had them puppies at nine months!"
171. "My dog needs his dismemberment shot." **I recommend against that.**
172. "I think my dog has Down's Syndrome."
173. Reason client doesn't want to spay: "My cat won't get pregnant because she only goes out during the day."
174. "He only coughs when he's at rest or when he's doing something."
175. Client intestinal parasite treatment: "Make the dog drink two watered-down beers."
176. "No, he's not on heartworm prevention. He runs too fast to get bit by mosquitos."
177. "My dog's never been vaccinated. I don't want him to get autism."
178. "Another vet told me those were "acid toast" lumps." (to ease your mind and after much confusing dialogue: acid toast = adipose)
179. "What percent pig is a Guinea pig?" **"The percent that isn't Guinea."**
180. "I didn't think I was supposed to give the medicine this morning, so I gave it."
181. "I thought animal teaspoons were different than people teaspoons."

182. An owner kept saying she gives her dog "peanut butter balls". After professing confusion the owner explained, "You know, for seizures." (peanut butter balls = phenobarbital)
183. "Can I get her neutered instead of spayed, because it's cheaper."
184. "I won't let any other doctor touch my Mickey." **Mickey is a dog you sick-minded people! And I'm the doctor thank you very much.**
185. "A vet told us he gets a green allergy in his ears from swimmin' in the lake." (green allergy = green algae)
186. About a cat: "He's strictly indoors. Except when he gets out."
187. "He's fine with everything, but don't touch his penis." **Right. Got it. No touchy the pee-pee.**
188. Regarding not doing dental cleaning: "I'll just catch squirrels, put toothpaste on them, and feed them to my dog."
189. When presented an estimate for tumor removal: "How much to just send it to the lab without removing it?"
190. "Beer kills intestinal parasites."
191. Given enough Albon to give for ten days of labeled dose, owner replied: "How do I know on which day to stop?"
192. "We don't need flea control because we have chickens."
193. "I think my bitch has mites in her fairy."
194. "I think he's emancipated." **I think he's emaciated, but I guess he could be emancipated as well.**
195. "I'm worried about my cat. He seems nostalgic." (nostalgic = lethargic)
196. "My Husky puppy doesn't need to be neutered because he's gay."
197. "He gets kind of aggressive when he's playing. Do you think it's because his mom ate some cocaine when she was pregnant?"
198. "If you've got a spray that makes toys smell like crotches….that's something I'd be interested in."
199. "Has she gone into heat? Oh, yeah. She loves the sun."
200. Different client than in above, this time with a cat: "Has she gone into heat? Yes, she likes to sit on the radiator."
201. "I think my dog might have hip dysphagia."
202. "I don't think we want to do a dental. She had a rough recovery from her spay when she was young. They said she had a problem with amnesia."
203. "My dog is slaverating a lot!" **"I see he's also salivating a lot too!"**
204. "My cat's not been using the litterbox. I think he has unitarian disease."
205. "I brought him in to get x-rated."

206. Dog brought in for itching: "I bathe him in Dawn all the time, so I know it isn't fleas." **"All Dawn does is make cleaner fleas."**

207. "He's allergic to steroids."

208. "My dog got parvo from my Mom's cat."

209. "I'm building a safe room in my house and I want to get tranquilizers for my dog so that if we have to use the safe room he won't use up all the oxygen."

210. Doing presurgical check-in and asking about having taken away food and water: "I did. But it's raining out, so I'm not sure if he got some of that in his mouth."

211. "I bought some treats that say they are chicken-flavored but they're shaped like fish. Are they ok to feed to my cat?"

212. "I don't want to do bloodwork. I just want you to tell me if he has a disease."

213. "I'm not able to pay my bill. I have a thyroid problem and when it flares up I get memory loss."

214. Owner scheduling a dog for limping: "Should I bring him with me for the exam?" **"No, that's not necessary. Just bring in the leg if that's all that's the problem."**

215. "We feed him peanuts in the shell to keep his anal glands under control."

Afterword

I hope you find this profession to be everything you thought it would be. My second hope is, if it isn't, that you are able to make it as great for yourself as possible. I fall firmly into the second category. The difficulties we have had to overcome to become veterinarians have been many. The difficulties we have to surmount every day can be overwhelming. My goal for this book has been to present some ideas in either prose or illustrated form that make the bumps and crevasses you traverse a bit smoother; a little emotional and intellectual shock absorber. I have presented how I approach the job and my way is certainly not the only approach. I hope you have found something to laugh over and hopefully something that has helped redefine your troubles. If nothing else, know you are not alone. We are all in the same boat and we are all here for each other.

I had a classmate in school who said none of us fail. He said we flail. Because we're always in there giving it our best, thrashing around, perhaps not in the most graceful or agile fashion, like the thirteenth round in boxing. We flail, but we don't truly fail. I think of that often when a day seems especially long and trying.

We are so knowledgeable about behavior and medicine. How to bandage wounds, repair fractures, balance hormones, positive reinforcement techniques, medications to alleviate or cure disease. And yet we don't practice that same level of devotion and commitment to our own mental and physical health. To continue to do anything in life, we need to attend to our needs just as well.

I find most of my fulfillment in life is completely apart from my job. The most trying part of my life is my job. However, my job allows me to do those other things. Perhaps tolerance of a job is all most of us can achieve. If the career isn't satisfying, find something that does that for you. If I can impose anything on you, Dear Reader who has shown such indulgence as to reach the end of this book, take care of yourself, don't be too hard on yourself. There are many people who care about you, even if you don't believe so. I don't know you, but if you're in this profession, I know what you've been through and what you're going through and *I care* about you. This book is a practice in sharing and I hope you can turn to it and find a kindred spirit, a virtual personality perhaps that assures you that you are okay. If you are struggling, reach out to others for help. Trust me, there are people just waiting to catch you should you feel like you're falling.

Keep on flailing, fellow veterinary brethren.

About the Author

Annette Docsway is a shy, reclusive veterinarian, rarely seen in the wild. Some say she is a myth since there are no reported pictures of her and only anecdotal stories. This book, of course, disproves that, but you will find her to be as furtive and elusive, as a Mewtwo Pokemon.

Her origins, as far as investigators have been able to determine, are her having been the sole progeny of two human beings who had no business being together. In sharp contradiction, she also has a brother and a sister who aren't related to each other. She is the only one of her siblings that pursued the veterinary profession, though her sister houses more cats and chickens than the law or sanitation standards of her state allow.

She did graduate from Arizona State University, though eschewed the actual ceremony. If ever pressed in public, she will not admit to her time spent in the bowels of the UCDavis Veterinary Correctional Institute as she still suffers from PVSD (Post-Vet School Disorder). UCDavis could not be reached for comment, saying only that the restraining order remains in place.

She has lived in several states, as liquid, gas, and solid. Her favorite state of mind is REM, riding those delta waves. She has been in the state of denial, but will not admit it. She has traveled extensively, as familiar with Maycomb, Alabama as Brantisvogan or Tralfamadore.

Dr. Docsway has been in private practice (principally cats and dogs) for over two decades now, though she doesn't like to use the word "practice" because she thinks she has it down pretty well now. And as to "private", it seems like there is never any privacy as people are in and out of there all day long. She blames unlocking the door every morning for that problem.

At the time of this writing, barring financial windfall, such as this book actually selling, she hopes to slide into her later-life narrative and senile reverie in about 4,168 days. She has not yet decided on post-vet life, trying to decide between recluse ala Greta Garbo or cautionary tale ala Joan of Arc, but is intent on notoriety in some manner.

Made in United States
Orlando, FL
21 September 2023